THE
U.S. HISTORY
COOKBOOK

DELICIOUS RECIPES AND
EXCITING EVENTS
FROM THE PAST

Joan D'Amico
Karen Eich Drummond, Ed.D., R.D.

Illustrations by Jeff Cline
and Tina Cash-Walsh

WILEY

John Wiley & Sons, Inc.

Published by John Wiley & Sons, Inc., Hoboken, New Jersey
Published simultaneously in Canada

Design and production by Navta Associates, Inc.

The publisher and the authors have made every reasonable effort to ensure that the experiments and activities in this book are safe when conducted as instructed but assume no responsibility for any damage caused or sustained while performing the experiments or activities in the book. Parents, guardians, and/or teachers should supervise young readers who undertake the experiments and activities in this book.

For general information about our other products and services, please contact our Customer Care Department within the United States at (800) 762-2974, outside the United States at (317) 572-3993 or fax (317) 572-4002.

Wiley also publishes its books in a variety of electronic formats. Some content that appears in print may not be available in electronic books. For more information about Wiley products, visit our web site at www.wiley.com.

Library of Congress Cataloging-in-Publication Data

D'Amico, Joan, date.
     The U.S. history cookbook : delicious recipes and exciting events from the past / Joan D'Amico and Karen Eich Drummond ; illustrations by Jeff Cline and Tina Cash-Walsh.
       p. cm.
    Summary: Chapters discuss different time periods in American history, focusing on typical foods and cooking styles. Includes recipes for such dishes as pumpkin bread, Virginia ham with cherry sauce, and buckwheat griddle cakes.
     ISBN 0-471-13602-6
     1. Cookery, American—Juvenile literature. 2. United States—History—Juvenile literature. [1. Cookery, American. 2. United States—History.] I. Drummond, Karen Eich. II. Cline, Jeff, ill. III. Cash-Walsh, Tina, 1960- ill. IV. Title.
TX715 .D18193 2003
641.5973—dc21

Printed in the United States of America

10 9 8 7 6 5 4 3 2 1

We would like to solemnly and respectfully dedicate this book to all of the families who lost loved ones on September 11, 2001, and to the American people who continue to make this the greatest nation in the world.

CONTENTS

ACKNOWLEDGMENTS

Thanks to Christi Leigh D'Amico, food preparation assistant.

ABOUT THIS BOOK

American history isn't just about important people, places, and events. It is also about what foods people ate and where they got their food. This book will help you explore the history of food along with the history of the United States. Each chapter discusses a different period in American history, tells you about typical foods and cooking styles of the time, and includes recipes you can make.

Just think of the places you'll go! Visit the Louisiana Territory and learn about Creole and Cajun foods. (Be sure to make the King Cake for the Mardi Gras Festival!) Ride with the cowboys in Texas and eat tacos and chili around the chuck wagon. Camp out with pioneers and cook up a real pioneer breakfast on the trail west. You'll dine on the transcontinental railroad, cook foods from your World War II victory garden, or eat Peace, Love, and Crunchy Granola from the 1960s.

Before you start this book, be sure to read the "Discovering the Kitchen" section that starts on page 3. It covers the basics on kitchen safety, utensils, cooking terms, and measuring. Each recipe lists how much time you will need to make it, the kitchen tools you'll need, and the number of servings it makes.

From the first Thanksgiving to the end of the twentieth century, we hope you appreciate the diversity and the cooking traditions of the people who have made American cooking as exciting as it is today. Enjoy your trip along the timeline of American food and cooking.

DISCOVERING THE KITCHEN

TOOLS OF THE TRADE

baking pan

colander

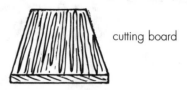
cutting board

biscuit cutter

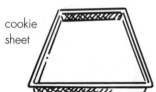

cookie sheet

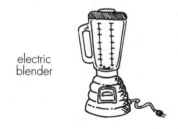

electric blender

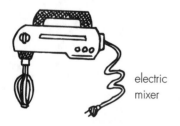

electric mixer

Let's take a close look at the cooking equipment in your kitchen. These are the basic tools you'll need to prepare the recipes in this book. Any kitchen tools that are used in only one or two recipes are described within those recipes.

baking pan   A square or rectangular pan used for baking and cooking foods in the oven. The most common sizes are 9 x 13-inch and 8-inch square.

biscuit cutter   A round outline, usually made from metal, used to cut biscuits from dough.

colander   A large perforated bowl used for rinsing food and draining pasta or other foods.

cookie sheet   A large rectangular pan with no sides or with half-inch sides, used for baking cookies and other foods.

cutting board   Made from wood or plastic, cutting boards provide a surface on which to cut foods.

egg separator   A small, shallow metal cup with slots used to separate the egg whites from the yolk. The yolk sits in the middle while the whites drop through the slots into a bowl.

electric blender   A glass or plastic cylinder with a rotating blade at the bottom. A small motor in the base turns the blade. The blender has different speeds and is used for mixing, blending, grinding, and pureeing.

electric mixer   Two beaters that rotate to mix ingredients together. Used for mashed potatoes, cake batters, and other mixing jobs.

grater   A metal surface with sharp-edged holes used for shredding and grating foods such as vegetables and cheese.

knives:

- **paring knife**   A knife with a small pointed blade used for trimming and paring vegetables and fruits and other cutting jobs that don't require a larger knife. (Most recipes in this book call for a knife. You will find the paring knife works well in most situations.)

- **peeler**   A handheld tool that removes the peel from fruits and vegetables.

- **sandwich spreader**   A knife with a dull blade that is designed to spread fillings on bread.

- **table knife**   A knife used as a utensil at the table.

layer cake pans   Round metal pans used to bake layers of a cake.

measuring cups   Cups with measurements (½ cup, ⅓ cup, etc.) on the side, bottom, or handle. Measuring cups that have spouts are used for liquid ingredients. Measuring cups without spouts are used for dry ingredients such as flour.

measuring spoons   Used for measuring small amounts of foods such as spices. They come in a set of 1 tablespoon, 1 teaspoon, ½ teaspoon, and ¼ teaspoon.

microwave dish   A dish that can safely be used in the microwave oven. The best microwave dishes say "microwave safe" on the label. Don't use metal pans, aluminum foil, plastic foam containers, brown paper bags, plastic wrap, or margarine tubs in the microwave.

mixing bowls   Round-bottomed bowls used for mixing and whipping all kinds of foods. Depending on the amount of ingredients, a large, medium, or small bowl may be used.

muffin tins   Metal or glass pans with small, round cups used for baking muffins and cupcakes.

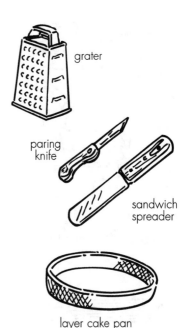

grater

paring knife

sandwich spreader

layer cake pan

measuring cup

measuring spoons

mixing bowl

muffin tin

frying pan

saucepan

pastry blender

rolling pin

rubber spatula

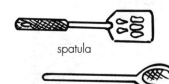

spatula

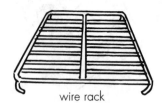

wooden spoon

tube pan

wire rack

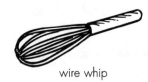

wire whip

pans:

- **frying pan** (also called a sauté pan)   Used for cooking foods, such as hamburgers or onions, in hot fat.

- **saucepan** (also called a pot)   Used for general stovetop cooking, such as boiling pasta or simmering a sauce.

pastry blender   A group of stiff wires attached to both ends of a handle. It is used, with a rocking motion, to blend butter or margarine into flour and other dry ingredients to make a dough.

rolling pin   A wooden or plastic roller used to flatten items such as pie crust and biscuit dough.

rubber spatula   A flat, flexible rubber or plastic tip on a long handle. It is used to scrape bowls, pots, and pans and for **folding** (a gentle over-and-under motion) ingredients into whipped cream or other whipped batter.

spatula   A flat metal or plastic tool used for lifting and turning meats, eggs, and other foods.

spoons:

- **teaspoon**   A spoon used for measuring. Also the name for the spoon normally used as a utensil at the table.

- **wooden spoon**   Used for mixing ingredients together and stirring.

tube pan   A metal cake pan with a center tube used for making angel food cakes, Bundt cakes, and special breads.

wire rack   Used for cooling baked goods.

wire whip   Used especially for whipping egg whites and cream.

COOKING SKILLS

Chefs need to master cutting and measuring skills and the basics of mixing and stovetop cooking. Here are the skills you will be practicing as you try the recipes in this book.

CUTTING

Foods are cut before cooking so that they will look good and cook evenly. Place the food to be cut on a cutting board and use a knife that is a comfortable size for your hand. To hold the knife, place your hand on top of the handle and fit your fingers around the handle. The grip should be secure but relaxed. In your other hand, hold the item being cut. Keep your fingertips curled under to protect them from cuts. (See the "Safety Rules" section on page 11 for more on how to cut safely.)

Here are some commonly used cutting terms you'll need to know:

chop To cut into irregularly shaped pieces.

dice To cut into cubes of the same size.

mince To chop very fine.

slice To cut into uniform slices.

Grating and shredding are also examples of cutting:

grate To rub a food across a grater's tiny punched holes to produce small or fine pieces of food. Hard cheeses and some vegetables are grated.

shred To rub a food across a surface with medium to large holes or slits. Shredded foods look like strips. The cheese used for making pizza is always shredded.

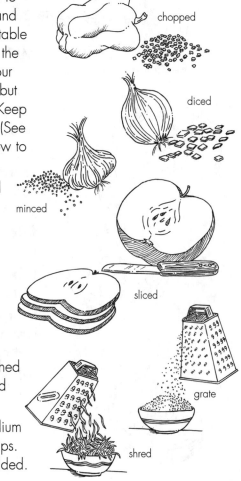

chopped

diced

minced

sliced

grate

shred

dry measurement

liquid measurement

beat

fold

whip

MEASURING

Ingredients can be measured in three different ways: by counting (six apples), by measuring volume (½ cup of applesauce), or by measuring weight (a pound of apples).

To measure the volume of a liquid, always place the measuring cup on a flat surface and check that the liquid goes up to the proper line on the measuring cup while you are looking directly at it at eye level.

To measure the volume of a dry ingredient, such as flour, spoon it into the measuring cup and level it off with a table knife. Do not pack the cup with the dry ingredient— that is, don't press down on it to make room for more—unless the recipe says to.

MIXING

There are all kinds of ways to mix! Here are definitions of the most common types.

beat   To move a utensil back and forth to blend ingredients together.

cream   To mix a solid fat (usually margarine or butter) and sugar by pressing them against a bowl with the back of a spoon until they look creamy.

fold   To move a utensil with a gentle over-and-under motion.

mix   To combine ingredients so that they are all evenly distributed.

whip   To beat rapidly using a circular motion, usually with a whip, to incorporate air into the mixture (such as in making whipped cream).

whisk   To beat ingredients together lightly with a wire whip until they are well blended.

STOVETOP COOKING

There are different ways to cook on your stove. Here are descriptions of cooking methods you will be practicing as you try the recipes in this book. Because it is easy to get burned while cooking on the stove, see the "Safety Rules" section on page 11.

boil   To heat a liquid to its boiling point, or to cook in a boiling liquid. Water boils at 212°F. You can tell it is boiling when you see lots of large bubbles popping to the surface. When a liquid boils, it is turning into steam (the gaseous state of water). Water can't get any hotter than 212°F; it can only make steam faster. Boiling is most often used for cooking pasta.

pan-fry   To cook in a pan over moderate heat in a small amount of fat. Hamburgers are an example of a food that can be pan-fried.

sauté   To cook quickly in a pan over medium-high heat in a small amount of fat. Vegetables, especially onions, are often sautéed in oil to bring out their flavor and brown them.

simmer   To heat a liquid to just below its boiling point, or to cook in a simmering liquid. You can tell a liquid is simmering when it has bubbles floating slowly to the surface. Most foods cooked in liquid are simmered. Always watch simmering foods closely so that they do not boil.

steam   To cook in steam. Steam has much more heat and cooks foods more quickly than boiling water does. Steaming is an excellent method for cooking most vegetables.

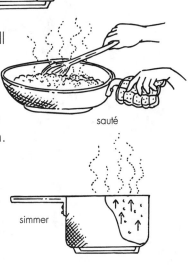

boil

sauté

simmer

CRACKING AND SEPARATING EGGS

It is best to crack an egg into a clear glass cup (such as a measuring cup) before adding it to the other ingredients. That way, if the egg smells bad or has a red spot, you can throw it out before the egg goes in with the other ingredients. An egg with a red spot is safe to eat but is usually thrown out because of its appearance. You should also remove any pieces of eggshell from the egg before adding the egg to the other ingredients.

Sometimes you will need to separate the egg yolk from the egg white for a recipe. To do this, crack the egg over an egg separator and a bowl. Make sure you get the yolk in the middle. The whites will drain out into the bowl. If you don't have an egg separator, you can separate an egg by cracking it over a bowl, keeping the yolk in one half of the shell. Carefully pass the egg yolk from one half of the shell to the other without letting it break until the white has fallen into the bowl.

SAFETY RULES

The kitchen can be a safe, or a very dangerous, part of your home. What's dangerous in your kitchen? Sharp knives, boiling water, and hot oil are a few things. Always check with an adult before trying any of the recipes. Talk to him or her about what you are allowed to do by yourself and when you need an adult's assistance. And always follow these safety guidelines.

AROUND THE STOVE AND OVEN

- Get an adult's permission before you use a stove or oven.
- Don't wear long, baggy shirts or sweaters when cooking. They could catch fire.
- Never turn your back on a frying pan that contains oil.
- Never fry with oil at a high temperature.
- Don't spray a pan with vegetable oil cooking spray over the stove or near heat. Oil will burn at high temperatures, so spray the pan over the sink.
- If a fire starts in a pan on the stove, you can smother it by covering it with the pan lid or pouring baking soda on it. Never use water to put out a fire in a pan with oil—it only makes a fire worse.
- Always use pot holders or wear oven mitts when using the oven or handling something that is hot. Make sure your pot holders are not wet. Wet pot holders transmit the heat from the hot item you are holding directly to your skin.
- Don't overfill pans with boiling or simmering liquids.
- Open pan lids away from you to let steam escape safely.

- Keep pan handles turned away from the edge of the stove. Knocking against them can splatter hot food.
- Stir foods with long-handled spoons.
- Keep pets and small children away from hot stoves and ovens during cooking. (Try to keep them out of the kitchen altogether.)

USING ANY APPLIANCE

- Use an appliance only if you know exactly how to operate it and you have permission from an adult.
- Never operate an appliance that is near the sink or sitting in water.
- Don't use frayed electrical cords or damaged plugs and outlets. Tell an adult.

USING A MICROWAVE OVEN

- Use only microwave-safe cookware, paper towels, paper plates, or paper cups.
- Use pot holders or oven mitts to remove items.
- If a dish is covered, make sure there is some opening through which steam can escape during cooking.
- When taking foods out of the microwave, you must open the container so that steam escapes *away* from your hands and face.
- Prick foods like potatoes and hot dogs with a fork before putting them into the microwave.
- Never try to cook a whole egg in the microwave—it will burst!

USING A KNIFE

- Get an adult's permission before using any knife.

- Always pick up a knife by its handle.

- Pay attention to what you're doing!

- Cut away from the body and away from anyone near you.

- Use a sliding, back-and-forth motion when slicing foods with a knife.

- Don't leave a knife near the edge of a table. It can be easily knocked off, or a small child may touch it.

- Don't try to catch a falling knife.

- Don't use knives to cut string, to open cans or bottles, or as a screwdriver.

- Don't put a knife into a sink full of water. Instead, put it on the drainboard, to avoid cutting yourself.

CLEANING UP

Whenever you use a knife and cutting board to cut meat, poultry, or seafood, be sure to wash them thoroughly before using them again. These foods contain germs that can be harmful, and you don't want the germs to get onto foods that won't be cooked, such as vegetables for salads.

CHAPTER 1

THE FIRST THANKSGIVING

One cold day late in November 1620, a British ship named the *Mayflower* laid anchor off the tip of Cape Cod in present-day Massachusetts. The *Mayflower* was supposed to land in what was called "Northern Virginia," but the ship landed farther north instead. The passengers on the *Mayflower* were mainly **Pilgrims** from England who wanted to separate from the Church of England. They had spent a hard two months at sea to get to the New World because they felt it was the one place where they could practice their religion as they wished.

In a short time, the Pilgrims established their settlement on the shores of nearby Plymouth Bay. The area around Plymouth Bay was once inhabited by the Patuxet tribe. However, the Native American tribe had all been wiped out by 1618 by disease (probably smallpox) carried by earlier European explorers.

FUN FOOD FACTS

- The Pilgrims didn't use forks. They used knives and spoons and also their hands to eat. Thankfully they brought along large napkins!
- Cranberries, which grew wild in wetlands areas, were first called "crane berries" because cranes tramping through the wetlands gobbled them up.
- Lobster wasn't always a delicacy. Residents of an early Maine settlement protested vigorously against being served lobster at every meal.

The first winter was very tough for the Pilgrims. They had only limited housing and food, and many died of malnutrition, exposure, and illness. Only half the original 102 settlers lived through to spring. In the spring, however, the Pilgrims' fortunes changed when they met Squanto, a member of the Patuxet who had grown up around Plymouth, but was kidnapped by an English captain and sold into slavery in Spain. Upon escaping from Spain, Squanto went to England where he was

able to get on a ship sailing to the New World. Unfortunately, when he returned to his old village, he discovered that his people had all died. Using the English he had learned from his captors, Squanto was able to show the Pilgrims how to plant corn, catch cod and herring, tap maple trees for their sweet sap, and trap deer and other **game** (wild animals that are hunted).

Squash, beans, and a type of corn called maize were very important crops for the Native Americans, and they became important to the Pilgrims and future colonists as well. Native Americans showed the Pilgrims how to plant five kernels of corn into a mound of soil. Then, when the corn stalks were two or three feet tall, beans and squash were planted around the stalks. The cornstalks supported these plants and shaded them from the hot summer sun. Native Americans then taught the Pilgrims how to harvest the corn, grind it into cornmeal, and use it in cooking and baking.

The Pilgrims' first autumn was beautiful and their harvest was plentiful, and they decided to have a harvest feast. The Plymouth 1621 harvest feast included lots of food, games, and ninety Native American guests. It probably took place in late September or early October. Squanto was asked to invite braves from the local Wampanoag tribe and their leader Massasoit to the feast. **Venison** (deer meat), goose, duck, wild turkey, lobster, Indian corn, wild grapes, and puddings were some of the featured foods.

Golden Harvest Pumpkin Bread

Time
25 to 30 minutes
to prepare
plus
1 hour to bake

Tools
5 × 8-inch loaf pan
dry and liquid
measuring cups
measuring spoons
2 medium bowls
sifter
wooden spoon
1 small bowl
fork
wire whip
zipper-lock plastic bag
rolling pin
rubber spatula
oven mitts
wire rack

Makes
1 loaf

The first Thanksgiving with the Pilgrims was an awesome feast, but we don't know much about the specific foods or dishes served. There certainly would have been pompion (pumpkin), but not in pompion pie. The pumpkins would probably have been stewed or boiled. Here's a way to make pumpkin a bit tastier.

Ingredients

vegetable oil cooking spray
1¾ cups all-purpose flour
¼ teaspoon baking powder
1 teaspoon baking soda
1 teaspoon salt
1 teaspoon ground cinnamon
¼ teaspoon ground nutmeg
⅓ cup margarine or butter

¾ cup sugar
2 eggs
1 cup canned pumpkin purée
⅓ cup low-fat or skim milk
1 teaspoon vanilla extract
½ cup pecans
½ cup raisins

Steps

1. Preheat the oven to 350°F. Spray the loaf pan with vegetable oil cooking spray.

2. In a medium bowl, sift together the flour, baking powder, baking soda, salt, cinnamon, and nutmeg. These are the dry ingredients.

3. In the other medium bowl, cream the margarine and sugar by pressing the ingredients against the bowl with the back of the wooden spoon until soft and fluffy.

4. Break the eggs in the small bowl, and mix with a fork. Add the eggs, pumpkin, milk, and vanilla and mix with the wire whip.

5. Place the pecans in the plastic bag and zip the bag closed, making sure all the air is gone. Crush the nuts by rolling the rolling pin over the bag several times until the texture is coarse.

6. Add the creamed mixture to the dry ingredients and stir together just until the ingredients are well moistened.

7. With the rubber spatula, fold in the raisins and pecans.

8. Pour the batter into the greased baking pan.

9. Bake for 1 hour, or until the bread is firm and deep golden brown. Using oven mitts, remove the bread from the oven.

10. Let the bread cool on the wire rack for 20 minutes. Turn the pan over onto the wire rack and shake gently to remove the bread.

Cornmeal Blueberry Mush, or Sautauthig (Sawf-taw-teeg)

Time
15 minutes

Tools
dry and liquid measuring cups

colander

measuring spoons

3-quart saucepan and lid

wooden spoon

wire whip

small bowl

Makes
9 ½-cup servings

This recipe was a favorite dish of the Native Americans of the Northeast. It was a simple pudding made with crushed dried blueberries, cracked corn (called samp), and water. Later, settlers added milk for additional richness. The Pilgrims loved sautauthig and many historians believe that it was part of the first Thanksgiving. Here is an updated version so you can try it too!

Ingredients

2 cups fresh blueberries	½ teaspoon salt
1½ cups low-fat or skim milk	3 tablespoons maple syrup
1½ cups water	½ teaspoon ground nutmeg
¾ cups cornmeal	1 tablespoon sugar

Steps

1. Put the blueberries in the colander and rinse them under running water. Gently pat them dry.

2. Combine the milk and water in the saucepan.

3. Set the saucepan over medium heat, and stir constantly with the wooden spoon until bubbles form around the edges of the pan.

4. Using the wire whip, slowly stir in the cornmeal and salt and whisk constantly until there are no lumps in the mixture.

5. Reduce the heat to low. Cover the saucepan and simmer for 10 minutes until thickened.

6. Turn off the heat and fold in the maple syrup and blueberries.

7. In the small bowl, mix together the nutmeg and sugar. Sprinkle on the top of the mush and serve immediately.

The Ultimate Roasted Turkey Breast

Turkey, ducks, geese, and venison (deer meat) were the main attractions of the first Thanksgiving feast.

Ingredients

3- to 4-pound turkey breast
1 tablespoon vegetable oil
1 teaspoon ground sage
1 teaspoon dried thyme
1 teaspoon dried rosemary
1 teaspoon paprika
½ teaspoon salt
¼ teaspoon ground black pepper

Steps

1. Preheat the oven to 325°F and remove the turkey breast from the package.

2. Rinse inside cavity of turkey breast under running water. Pat dry with paper towels.

3. Place breast skin side up on the rack in the roasting pan.

4. Using the pastry brush, brush the turkey with the vegetable oil.

5. In the small bowl, mix together the sage, thyme, rosemary, paprika, salt, and pepper.

6. Sprinkle the spices on the turkey.

7. Place the turkey on the center rack in the oven and roast for 1½ to 2 hours. To check for doneness you will need a meat thermometer. Insert the meat thermometer into the thickest part of breast without touching the bone. The meat is done when the temperature on the thermometer reaches 170°F.

8. When finished, take the turkey out of the oven with oven mitts. Let the meat rest for a few minutes.

9. Have an adult help you carve with a serrated knife on a cutting board.

Time
10 minutes to prepare
plus
1½ to 2 hours
to cook

Tools
paper towels
roasting pan with rack
measuring spoons
pastry brush
small bowl
wooden spoon
meat thermometer
oven mitts
serrated knife
cutting board

Makes
4 to 5 servings

···· Traditional Cranberry Sauce ····

Time
20 minutes to prepare
plus
2 hours to chill

Tools
dry and liquid
measuring cups

measuring spoons

colander

paper towels

3-quart saucepan

wooden spoon

heatproof bowl

Makes
8 ¼-cup servings

Berries and dried fruits were considered delicacies and were a main part of the first Thanksgiving feast. The Pilgrims may have made cranberry sauce sweetened with maple syrup instead of sugar. Cranberries, which grew in wet swamps and marshes, were plentiful in the area. Native Americans also picked and ate cranberries, and used them to make pemmican. Pemmican, often referred to as "trail cake," was made of dried meat that had been pounded into a powder, fat such as deer fat, and dried cranberries or other dried berries. Pemmican was an easy-to-carry nutritious food that was always ready to eat.

Ingredients

½ pound cranberries

1 cup sugar

1 cup water

⅛ teaspoon salt

Steps

1. Wash the cranberries in the colander, then pat dry with paper towels. Pick out any cranberries that are bruised or green.

2. In the saucepan, mix the sugar, water, and salt together with the wooden spoon. Place on top of the stove over low heat and stir until the sugar is dissolved.

3. Bring the sugar mixture to a low boil. Ask an adult to add the cranberries to the pan.

4. Boil the cranberries for 5 minutes or until all of the skins stop popping.

5. Turn off the heat and allow the cranberry sauce to cool in the pan for 10 minutes.

6. Transfer the sauce to the heatproof bowl and refrigerate for at least 2 hours.

CHAPTER 2

COLONIAL FARE

S pain, France, England, and the Netherlands all set up colonies in North America. A **colony** is a territory outside the borders of a country that is claimed and controlled by that country. The Spanish were the first, establishing colonies in Florida, Texas, New Mexico, Arizona, and California. The French staked their claim to what is now Canada. England tried several times to establish North American colonies in the late 1500s and early 1600s, but failed. Then, in 1607 the Jamestown colony was founded in Virginia, and in 1620 the Plymouth colony was founded (as described in chapter 1). Soon thereafter, Massachusetts Bay and many other colonies were established and began to thrive.

England's first settlements along the Atlantic coast eventually became a string of thirteen colonies with French Canada to the north and Spanish Florida to the south. Many Europeans came to the colonies to practice their religion freely or to find work, land, or wealth. Some were servants

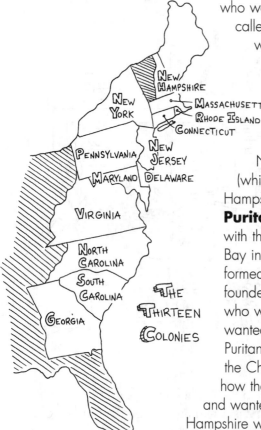

New Hampshire
New York
Massachusetts
Rhode Island
Connecticut
Pennsylvania
New Jersey
Maryland **Delaware**
Virginia
North Carolina
South Carolina
Georgia

The Thirteen Colonies

who were brought either by force or by a system called **indenture,** in which a person agreed to work for a certain period in return for room, board, and passage to the New World.

The thirteen British colonies were not united, and were often considered to fall into three distinct groups: New England, Middle Atlantic, and Southern colonies. The New England colonies were Massachusetts (which included what is now Maine), New Hampshire, Connecticut, and Rhode Island. **Puritans,** who like the Pilgrims had disagreements with the Church of England, settled in Massachusetts Bay in 1630. In 1636, Puritans in Connecticut formed the Connecticut Colony. Rhode Island was founded by Roger Williams, a Massachusetts minister who was expelled by the Puritans because he wanted more religious freedom. Even though the Puritans came to America to be free from the rules of the Church of England, they were very strict about how they practiced their religion in their new home and wanted everyone to follow their rules. New Hampshire was founded in 1623 when several Englishmen were given a land grant to establish a fishing colony at the mouth of the Piscataqua River.

New England colonists made their living mainly by fishing, whaling, shipbuilding, and farming, but farming was harder in New England than in the other colonies. The soil was often rocky and the growing season was shorter because of the longer winters.

The Middle Atlantic colonies included New York (acquired from the Dutch in 1664), New Jersey, Pennsylvania, and Delaware. Pennsylvania was founded in 1681 by William Penn, a Quaker. William Penn wanted a place where the

Quakers could practice their Protestant religion. Many German immigrants, especially farmers, settled in Pennsylvania. In 1638, newcomers from Sweden founded the colony of New Sweden in an area that would later become the colonies of Delaware and New Jersey.

The Middle Atlantic colonies had better soil and climate for farming than the New England colonies. The Middle Atlantic colonies were also known for crafts such as glassmaking.

The Southern colonies included Maryland, Virginia, North and South Carolina, and Georgia. The English established their first permanent colony in America in 1607 in Jamestown, Virginia. The colony struggled for the first few years, but eventually began to thrive as a center of agriculture. Maryland was founded in 1632 by Lord Baltimore to establish a safe home for English Catholics. Settlers from Virginia founded the colony of North Carolina around 1650. In 1670, a permanent English settlement was established on the coast of South Carolina near present-day Charleston. Georgia was founded by an Englishman named James Oglethorpe in 1733 as a home for the "worthy poor" of London.

Southern land was ideal for agriculture. Both large plantations and small farms grew crops such as tobacco and rice that were exported. African slaves were brought to to the southern colonies to do much of the farming on large plantations.

The meals of the colonists often included traditional English foods, such as meat, cheese, and butter, and Native American foods, such as beans and corn. Corn was a common ingredient in colonial cooking. When ground into cornmeal, it could be moistened with water or buttermilk and fried on a hot griddle to make journeycakes, or johnnycakes. Boiled with milk, cornmeal became corn mush or hasty pudding. (Hasty pudding got its name because it was quick and easy to make.) Corn was also served in Indian pudding, roasted in its husk over hot coals, or steamed over hot stones in an outdoor cooking pit. Southern colonists liked hominy, corn that was soaked in water and ashes. The soaking caused the corn to lose its outer skin and changed its flavor. The corn was then left whole or ground into a type of

FUN FOOD FACTS

- Honeybees were brought to Massachusetts in the 1600s. Their honey was used to sweeten foods and they also helped to pollinate many crops, especially apples.

- During colonial times, popular beverages included peach and apple cider. Not many families were fortunate enough to have a cow, so milk was not as common as nowadays.

- On Sunday, colonial families often ate baked beans. On Saturday night, the mother would put beans, molasses (for sweetness), and salt pork (for flavor) into a large pot. The beans would cook all night in the fireplace and be ready to eat on Sunday, after the family had been to church.

cornmeal called **grits.** Beans, squash, and pumpkins were also grown, along with other vegetables.

Colonists from Massachusetts to Georgia ate seafood from the ocean and rivers, as well as deer, turkey, goose, rabbit, and pork. They also used the fruits, herbs, and nuts they found in the countryside. Wild fruits included strawberries, blackberries, raspberries, blueberries, huckleberries, and grapes. If a family was fortunate enough to own a cow, they could make butter and cheese from its fresh milk. Foods that did not grow in the colonies, such as sugar or tea, were shipped from England or other countries and were quite expensive.

For sweetness, colonists often used maple syrup (from maple trees) or molasses, which was imported from the West Indies. Molasses was the major sweetener used in America until the 1900s because it was less expensive than sugar. Molasses was commonly used to make doughnuts, pies, cakes, cookies, corn bread, and baked beans.

Each cultural group brought their own food traditions with them. Well-to-do English colonists continued their tradition of having tea in the middle of the afternoon. The Dutch made waffles, cookies, cakes, crullers, and doughnuts. The Germans living in Pennsylvania brought cabbage, rye bread, and sausage with them. African slaves brought seeds of African plants, such as black-eyed peas, okra, sesame seeds, and peanuts.

Cooking was done over an open fire or in ovens heated by firewood. Most houses had a fireplace big enough to walk into. The fireplace was used both for cooking and for heating the home, and it usually had a big pot hung on an iron hook over the open fire. Also used were three-legged pots that stood directly over the fire. The pot was used for making stews, a very common meal that included whatever meat, vegetables, and herbs were available. There were no refrigerators. Vegetables were dried, and meat was dried, smoked, or salted to keep it from going bad.

•••••••••••• •••• Corn Chowder •••• ••••••••••••

Time
45 to 50 minutes

Tools
liquid measuring cup
measuring spoons
cutting board
paring knife
medium bowl
vegetable peeler
large pot
wooden spoon
wire whip

Makes
6 servings

A **chowder** is a thick soup made with fish, shellfish, and/or vegetables. Most chowders also contain milk and potatoes. Fish chowder was popular among many coastal Native American tribes.

Ingredients

1	onion	3	cups milk
2	medium baking potatoes	¼	teaspoon dried thyme
2	tablespoons butter	½	teaspoon dried parsley
2	tablespoons all-purpose flour	1	teaspoon salt
1	cup chicken broth	½	teaspoon white pepper
1	10-ounce package frozen corn		

Steps

1. On the cutting board, peel the papery skin off the onion and cut the onion in half. Dice the onion into small pieces and place them in the bowl.

2. Use the peeler to peel the outer skin off the potatoes. Cut the potatoes into cubes on the cutting board.

3. Preheat the pot over medium heat. Add the butter and let it melt. Add the onions and sauté them over medium heat until translucent.

4. Sprinkle the flour over the onions and stir with a wooden spoon until the flour bubbles and smells fragrant. This takes about 2 minutes.

5. Add the chicken broth to the onion mixture, stirring constantly with a wire whip until the chicken broth begins to boil.

6. Add the corn, potatoes, milk, thyme, parsley, salt, and pepper. Cook for about 20 minutes until the potatoes are tender.

Virginia Ham with Cherry Sauce

Virginia has been famous since colonial times for its ham. Virginia ham gets its special flavor from the peanuts that are fed to the hogs as well as from how the hams are prepared. The hams are first allowed to absorb salt (this is called "curing"), and then placed over fires of hickory or oak wood to absorb the woodsmoke flavor (this is called "smoking"). Finally the hams are rubbed with pepper and hung to age for at least six months (this is called "aging").

Ingredients

¾-pound boneless, cooked Virginia ham, sliced

3 tablespoons brown sugar

4 teaspoons cornstarch

¼ teaspoon ground cinnamon

1 cup apple juice

1 tablespoon vinegar

1 16-ounce can pitted tart red cherries packed in water, drained

Steps

1. Preheat the oven to 350°F.

2. Wrap the ham in foil. Place the ham in the oven to heat for 30 minutes.

3. While the ham is heating, get the ingredients ready to make the cherry sauce.

4. About 10 minutes before the ham is warmed up, make the sauce. In the saucepan, mix together the brown sugar, cornstarch, and cinnamon. Stir in the apple juice and vinegar. Cook, stirring frequently, over medium heat until the sauce is thick and bubbly.

5. Cook the sauce 2 more minutes. Stir in the cherries. Cook for 4 more minutes, or until the cherries are heated through.

6. Remove the foil-wrapped ham from the oven, using oven mitts. Place the ham on plates and ladle sauce over the ham.

Time
30 minutes

Tools
aluminum foil
liquid measuring cup
measuring spoons
medium saucepan
wooden spoon
oven mitts

Makes
4 servings

Old-Fashioned Dried Apple Rings

Time
15 minutes to prepare
plus
2 weeks to dry

Tools
vegetable peeler

apple corer

cutting board

paring knife

1 yard kitchen string

Makes
About 2 dozen pieces

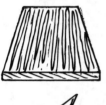

About ten years after the Pilgrims arrived in Plymouth, they started harvesting apples. The English loved apples and brought tree stock from England to grow in America. During colonial times, fresh apples were often dried so they could be eaten at other times of the year.

Ingredients

2   Granny Smith apples

Steps

1. Peel the apples with the vegetable peeler.

2. On the cutting board, use the corer to cut out a cylinder through the center of the apples, removing the stem and seeds.

3. Place the apples on their sides and slice them into ¼-inch rings.

4. Run the string through the hole in the center of each apple ring.

5. Hang the apple rings in a cool, dry place. Make sure the apple slices have room between them for the air to circulate.

6. Once the apples are wrinkled and dried, usually in two weeks, you can take them down and eat them. Store the remaining snacks in a covered container.

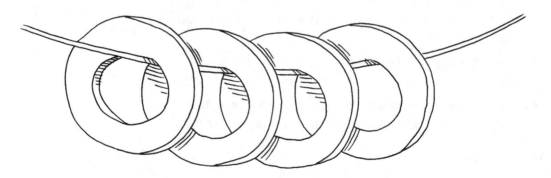

···· All-American Baked Apple ···· Crisp with Dried Fruits

Apples grew very well in the New England and Middle Atlantic colonies. The Dutch people who lived in New York especially liked to make pastries with apples. This recipe uses both fresh apples and dried fruits. You can use the dried apples made in the previous recipe if you wish. Colonists often made pie from dried fruits during the winter.

Filling Ingredients

4   Granny Smith apples
1   cup assorted dried fruits
½ cup sugar
1   teaspoon ground cinnamon

1   teaspoon ground nutmeg
½ teaspoon ground cloves
1   tablespoon all-purpose flour
vegetable oil cooking spray

Topping Ingredients

½ cup all-purpose flour
½ cup firmly packed brown sugar
1   teaspoon vanilla extract
4   tablespoons (½ stick) butter,

softened
½ cup pecans
1   teaspoon confectioners' sugar
vanilla ice cream (optional)

Time
25 minutes to prepare plus
1 hour to bake

Tools
dry measuring cups
measuring spoons
vegetable peeler
apple corer
cutting board
paring knife
2 medium bowls
wooden spoon
9-inch square baking pan
pastry blender
zipper-lock plastic bag
rolling pin
oven mitts
wire rack

Makes
16 servings

Steps

1. Preheat the oven to 350°F.

2. Peel and core the apples. Cut the apples in half on the cutting board. With cut side down, slice the apples into wedges. Place in a medium bowl.

3. Add the dried fruits, sugar, cinnamon, nutmeg, cloves, and 1 tablespoon of flour to the bowl with the apples. Stir with a wooden spoon.

4. Spray the baking pan with vegetable oil cooking spray and place the apple mixture in the pan.

5. In the other bowl, mix together ½ cup flour, the brown sugar, and vanilla extract with a wooden spoon.

6. Cut the butter into the mixture with the pastry blender, using a back and forth motion until the mixture looks like small peas.

7. Sprinkle the flour mixture evenly over the apples until all of the apples are covered.

8. Place the pecans in the plastic bag and seal it, making sure to press all of the air out of the bag. Crush the pecans into small pieces by rolling the rolling pin over the bag. Sprinkle pecans on the top of the flour mixture.

9. Bake the crisp for 1 hour until the topping is golden brown and the apples are bubbly.

10. Using oven mitts, remove the pan from the oven. Cool on a rack for 20 minutes.

11. Sprinkle with confectioners' sugar when cooled slightly. Serve the crisp with vanilla ice cream if you like.

CHAPTER 3
LOUISIANA TERRITORY CREOLE AND CAJUN FOODS

In 1776, the colonies won their independence from Britain and became the first thirteen United States. The late 1700s through the early 1800s became a period of great westward expansion, beginning just to the east of the Mississippi River, in what became Kentucky, Tennessee, and Ohio. West of the Mississippi River was the Louisiana Territory which Spain had owned since 1762. The Mississippi River was an important waterway, so the United States got Spain to sign a treaty in 1795 to guarantee Americans the right to use the Mississippi River. This treaty also opened the land on the east side of the lower Mississippi to American settlement.

In 1800, Spain made a deal giving the Louisiana Territory to France. President Thomas Jefferson was concerned that the French would not be as willing as Spain to allow Americans to navigate the Mississippi River, especially the lower Mississippi River. President Jefferson offered to purchase Florida, which at that time ran all the way up to the lower Mississippi River, from the French emperor Napoleon Bonaparte. Instead, Napoleon offered him the entire Louisiana Territory for $15 million. This offer was readily accepted. With the purchase of the Louisiana Territory in 1803, the United States more than doubled in size. Jefferson commissioned Meriwether Lewis and William Clark to explore and make maps of much of this new land, which extended from the Gulf of Mississippi west to the Rocky Mountains and north to Canada.

New Orleans was a very important city on the lower Mississippi River that the United States now owned. The French founded and named the city of New Orleans in 1718. Then, in 1762 the French government gave the land to the Spanish. The Spanish colony prospered. Shortly after Spain took control, French settlers who had been forced out of Canada by the British started arriving in the New Orleans area. These settlers were called Acadians because many came from Nova Scotia, which they called Acadie. Over the years, Acadian came to be pronounced **Cajun.** Cajuns speak their own dialect of French.

The foods and cooking of New Orleans in the early 1800s reflected the influences of the Native Americans of this area, the Cajuns, the ancestors of the original French and Spanish settlers (called **Creoles**), and the slaves who came from Africa and the West Indies. The most prevalent cooking styles are Creole and Cajun cooking. Both were influenced by the Native Americans. In addition, some Creole foods and ingredients have African

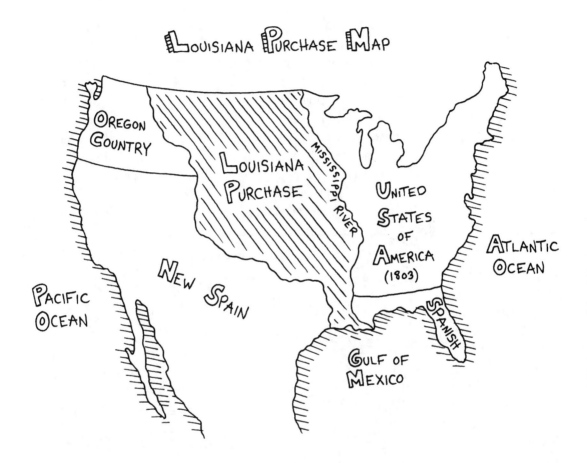

Louisiana Purchase Map

Oregon Country

Louisiana Purchase

Mississippi River

United States of America (1803)

New Spain

Spanish

Pacific Ocean

Atlantic Ocean

Gulf of Mexico

roots because Africans married into Creole families, and also because some families had African slaves as cooks.

Typical Creole dishes include spicy stews served with rice, such as gumbo and jambalaya. **Gumbo** is a thick, spicy soup usually thickened with **okra,** a green vegetable that came from Africa. The name "gumbo" comes from the African word for okra. Gumbo also usually includes seafood, sausage, and vegetables. **Crawfish,** which look like small lobsters and are native to the area, are a common ingredient in Creole and Cajun cooking.

Cajun cooking tends to be spicier than Creole cooking. Typical Cajun dishes include **boudin,** a highly seasoned sausage made with pork, shrimp, or crawfish; rice; onions; peppers; and herbs and spices. Cajun cooks use many kinds of peppers, especially hot ones. Onion, garlic, okra, paprika, and cumin (a strong spice) are also common. A favorite Cajun food is **pain perdu,** which means "lost bread" in French. When bread became stale, Cajuns turned it into this delicious dish resembling what we call French toast. The original pain perdu was flavored with orange-flower water.

FUN FOOD FACTS

- During Lewis and Clark's expedition in the new territory, the explorers found many fruits and vegetables they had never seen before, such as the Osage orange. The Osage orange tree was the first tree to be sent east by Lewis and Clark Unfortunately, its fruit was only edible to squirrels and other animals.

- The French enjoyed eating broiled beef steaks, but the beef in Louisiana was too tough to be broiled. Instead, they cut beef steaks into cubes and cooked them in gravy.

- Early French colonists are credited with bringing the **beignet** to New Orleans. A beignet is a square doughnut or fritter that is covered with powered sugar.

···· Shrimp and Ham Jambalaya ····

Jambalaya is a dish that the early Spanish contributed to New Orleans cooking. The name of this dish comes from the Spanish word for ham. The ingredients in jambalaya vary, but always include pork (ham or bacon) and shrimp. It often includes crawfish, too.

Time
15 minutes to prepare
plus
25 minutes to cook

Tools
dry and liquid
measuring cups

measuring spoons

cutting board

paring knife

large pot or Dutch
oven and lid

wooden spoon

Makes
6 servings

Ingredients

2   stalks celery

1   medium onion

1   clove garlic

¼   pound cooked ham or Canadian bacon

2   tablespoons margarine

⅛   teaspoon cayenne pepper

1   16-ounce can crushed tomatoes, undrained

1   6-ounce can tomato paste

⅓   cup water

1   teaspoon Worcestershire sauce

½   teaspoon salt

1   cup cooked rice

1   pound frozen shrimp, thawed

Steps

1. Wash and dry the celery. On the cutting board, cut each stalk in half lengthwise, then cut into small pieces.

2. Remove the papery skin from the onion. Cut the onion in half. Lay the halves flat side down on the board and chop into small pieces.

3. Peel and slice the garlic clove.

4. Dice the ham into ¼-inch pieces.

5. Preheat the pot or Dutch oven on medium heat for 2 minutes.

6. Melt the margarine in the bottom of the pot. Add the celery, onions, and garlic and cook until the vegetables are tender, about 3 minutes. Sprinkle with the cayenne pepper.

7. Add the crushed tomatoes, tomato paste, water, Worcestershire sauce, and salt to the pot. Stir with a wooden spoon. Cover and simmer for 15 minutes.

8. Add the cooked rice, shrimp, and ham to the pot. Cook, uncovered, for an additional 5 minutes.

9. Serve in bowls.

Bread Pudding with Fruit

Bread pudding is a traditional New Orleans dessert with French roots.

Ingredients

vegetable oil cooking spray

5 slices wheat or white bread

1 19-ounce can crushed pineapple

½ cup raisins

½ cup pecans

4 eggs

2 cups low-fat or skim milk

½ cup sugar

¼ teaspoon salt

1½ teaspoons vanilla extract

¼ teaspoon almond extract (optional)

3 tablespoons margarine

Steps

1. Preheat the oven to 350°F. Spray the baking pan with vegetable oil cooking spray.

2. On the cutting board, cut off the crusts of the bread, then cut the bread slices into cubes.

3. Place half the bread cubes in the baking pan.

4. Using the colander, drain the liquid from the pineapple. Spoon the pineapple over the bread cubes in the pan.

5. Place the remaining bread cubes on top of the pineapple, and sprinkle the raisins on top of the bread cubes.

6. Place the pecans into the plastic bag and zip it closed, pushing all the air out of the bag. Using a back and forth motion, roll the rolling pin over the pecans until they are crushed. Sprinkle the pecans over the raisins.

7. Separate the egg yolks from the egg whites using an egg separator.

8. In the bowl, mix together the egg yolks, milk, sugar, salt, vanilla extract, and the almond extract with the wire whip.

Time
35 minutes to prepare
plus
35 to 40 minutes
to bake

Tools
9-inch square baking pan
cutting board
paring knife
colander
wooden spoon
dry and liquid
measuring cups
measuring spoons
zipper-lock plastic bag
rolling pin
egg separator
medium bowl
wire whip
hand-held electric mixer
microwave dish
oven mitts

Makes
12 servings

9. Melt the margarine in the microwave dish in the microwave at full power for 30 seconds or until it turns to a liquid. Add it to the milk mixture and pour over the fruit, nuts, and bread cubes.

10. Bake for 35 to 40 minutes, or until a knife inserted in the center of the bread pudding comes out clean. Remove from the oven with oven mitts and allow to cool slightly.

11. Cut into squares and serve warm.

····King Cake····

New Orleans is famous for a festival called Mardi Gras. The tradition of Mardi Gras came from Paris where it has been celebrated since the Middle Ages. Mardi Gras, which is French for Fat Tuesday, is held on the Tuesday before the Christian holiday called Ash Wednesday. Ash Wednesday marks the beginning of Lent, the period before Easter when Catholics fast. Mardi Gras is a day of parades, parties, masks, and feasting, especially on King Cake. The King Cake is an oval-shaped cake decorated in the three Mardi Gras colors of purple, green, and gold. Inside the cake is a tiny plastic baby. The person who gets the piece with the baby is supposed to supply the King Cake at the next Mardi Gras. In this cake, you will use a pecan half instead of a plastic baby.

Time
15 minutes to prepare
plus
3 hours to rise
plus
30 minutes to bake

Tools
2 large mixing bowls
dry and liquid measuring cups
measuring spoons
3-quart saucepan
instant-read thermometer
2 wooden spoons
cutting board
pastry brush
kitchen towel
baking sheet
oven mitts
wire rack
small bowl
sifter
spatula

Makes
12 servings

Cake Ingredients

3¾ cups all-purpose flour

1 package active dry yeast

½ cup low-fat or skim milk

⅓ cup sugar

¼ cup (½ stick) margarine

½ teaspoon salt

3 eggs

½ cup chocolate minichips

½ cup chopped candied citron or golden raisins

1 tablespoon vegetable oil

1 pecan half

vegetable oil cooking spray

Icing Ingredients

1 cup confectioners' sugar

½ teaspoon vanilla extract

2 tablespoons low-fat or skim milk

2 tablespoons green colored sugar

2 tablespoons gold or yellow colored sugar

2 tablespoons purple colored sugar

Steps

1. In a large mixing bowl, combine 1½ cups flour with the yeast.

2. In the saucepan over medium heat, heat the milk, sugar, margarine, and salt until it is *lukewarm* and the margarine is melted (about 115°F). Check the temperature with a instant-read thermometer if available.

3. Add the milk mixture and eggs to the flour mixture. Stir with a wooden spoon until mixed well.

4. Add 2 cups flour to the bowl and mix. Form a ball of dough with your hands. Add the chocolate minichips and the candied citron.

5. Sprinkle 3 tablespoons of flour onto the cutting board. Knead the dough on the board by pressing the palm of your hand into the center, then folding the dough in half. Give the dough a quarter turn after each fold and start again. Knead for 6 to 8 minutes.

6. Using the pastry brush, grease the other large bowl with vegetable oil. Place the dough in the bowl and turn it once to oil the surface. Cover the bowl with a clean kitchen towel and let the dough rise in a warm place until it has doubled in size. This takes about 2 hours.

7. When you can poke your finger in the dough without the dough springing back, it has doubled in size. Pull the dough up on all sides, fold it over the center, and press down.

8. Press the pecan half into the center of the dough. Shape the dough into a 30-inch-long log. Make the dough into an oval shape and press the ends together.

9. Spray the baking sheet with vegetable oil cooking spray. Place the cake onto the cookie sheet and cover again with the towel. Let the cake rise for 1 hour.

10. Preheat the oven to 350°F. Bake the cake for 30 minutes or until it is golden brown. Using oven mitts, remove the cake from the oven and cool on a wire rack.

11. To make the icing, sift the confectioners' sugar into the small bowl.

12. Add the vanilla extract and the milk to the sugar and stir with a wooden spoon.

13. Spread the icing onto the cooled cake.

14. Sprinkle the colored sugar in two-inch rows on the top of the icing. First, use green. Next use gold or yellow. Last use purple.

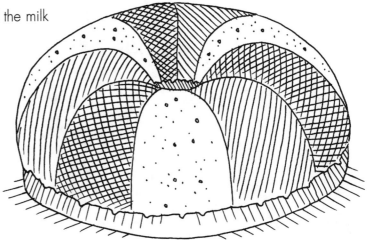

CHAPTER 4

REMEMBER (THOSE GREAT TORTILLAS AT) THE ALAMO!

Spain ruled the land from Mexico to California for over 300 years. When first exploring the area now known as Texas in the 1500s, Spanish explorers had met a Native American tribe whose word for friends was "tejas." The explorers changed the word to Texas and gave this name to the region. The Spanish did not establish settlements in Texas until the early 1700s, but these settlements grew quickly. After an eleven-year war with Spain that ended in 1821, Mexico won its independence and inherited Texas and all the other Spanish land that stretched to the Pacific Ocean.

In 1825, Mexico gave land in Texas to American land agents and American settlers began pouring in. Soon Americans outnumbered Mexicans in Texas. Some of the American settlers brought their slaves, which created a problem because Mexico did not allow slavery. In 1830, Mexico forbid further emigration into Texas by American settlers, and in 1835, the Texans began to revolt against Mexican rule. Less than a year later, Texas proclaimed its independence from Mexico. Mexico responded by sending in its army. A terrible battle was fought at the Alamo, an

FUN FOOD FACTS

- While a group of cowboys drove their herd north, the chuck wagon (which carried the cook and all the supplies for the cowboys' meals) would go ahead of the herd and stop where the cowboys planned to camp for the night. Then, the cook would set up camp and make dinner, often a beef stew with beans and chili peppers, and biscuits. Chuck wagon cooks were called a number of slang terms, such as stew builder, dough-belly, and hash slinger.

- The first commercial chili powder was developed in San Antonio, Texas. Chili powder is used to make a true Texan dish called **chili,** made from beef, chili peppers, and tomatoes.

- A common food for the Native American tribes in Texas was the pecan, a tasty nut that grows on trees. The pecan tree is now the state tree of Texas.

old Spanish church in San Antonio that the Americans had turned into a fort. Only 189 Texans were at the Alamo trying to defend it against a Mexican Army of more than 2,000 men. All of the Texans were killed. The bloody Battle of the Alamo infuriated people in the United States. Texas offered American settlers free land if they helped fight for independence. The new recruits, led by Sam Houston, helped defeat the Mexican army in the Battle of San Jacinto about six weeks later. Their rallying cry was "Remember the Alamo!"

Texas applied to be admitted into the United States of America, but it was not admitted until 1845. The Mexican government warned the United States that this would lead to war, which it did in 1846. The Mexicans finally admitted defeat in 1848, and gave Texas and all their other land except Mexico to the United States for $15 million.

The food and cooking of Texas was heavily influenced by the Spanish and Native Americans. The Native Americans of the southwest hunted deer, antelope, bison, and small game, and gathered wild fruits and nuts. They grew corn, beans, chili peppers, and other vegetables. When the Spanish arrived, they brought cattle, hogs, and sheep. The Spanish added Native American foods such as corn, chili peppers, beans, and tomatoes to their diet of beef, pork, and cheeses.

Early American settlers came mostly from the southern United States. They raised some cattle, hunted game, and grew corn, sweet potatoes, rye, and other crops. Most of these early Texans ate a lot of corn—fresh when it was in season, dried corn when it wasn't in season, and cornmeal at any time of year. Dried corn could be boiled before eating or ground into cornmeal. Cornmeal was used to make a hot cereal called corn mush, a type of pancake often called **johnnycakes,** and corn tortillas. The corn tortilla was the common bread of Texas. A stack of tortillas was served at every meal. Texans also learned to soak dried corn in limewater to make hominy. Hominy is then ground to make a type of corn flour called masa.

Cowboys on Texas ranches drove cattle to markets where they were sold for beef. The first herds were small and made of wild cattle that became the basis over time for the famous breed of Texas cattle called the **Texas longhorn.** The Texas longhorns were hardy animals that survived in the unforgiving climate of the Texas prairie. About a dozen cowboys would manage a herd of 2,500 Texas longhorns. Every fall, the cowboys would round up the cattle and brand each one with the ranch's symbol. After watching over the animals in the winter, the cowboys would drive them to markets over 1,000 miles away. Although Texas had lots of grass for the cattle to eat, the market for beef was mostly in the eastern United States. When trains became more common after the Civil War, long cattle drives became less frequent as the cowboys took the cattle to the nearest railroad town.

Mexican dishes, such as **tamales,** were popular in the cities and towns in the south of Texas. A tamale is made by spreading a cornmeal dough on a corn husk, then topping the dough with a spicy meat filling. The corn husk is then sealed and steamed so the inside cooks. Many meals were flavored with chili peppers. Cooks crushed the peppers with a little water and made a sauce that was fiery hot.

···· Awesome Tacos ····

Time
30 minutes

Tools
dry measuring cups
measuring spoons
paring knife
cutting board
large frying pan
wooden spoon
colander
medium heatproof bowl
microwave plate
(optional)
paper towel (optional)

Makes
6 servings (2 each)

Tacos are made with soft tortillas or crisp taco shells. The tortilla or taco is filled with meat or poultry and beans and then topped with lettuce, tomato, shredded cheese, and taco sauce.

Ingredients

1   small onion
1   tomato
1   tablespoon olive oil
1   pound lean ground beef, ground chicken, or ground turkey
2   teaspoons chili powder

1   teaspoon cumin
1   teaspoon dried parsley
12 corn tortillas or taco shells
1   cup chopped lettuce
1   cup shredded cheese
½   cup taco sauce

Steps

1. Remove the outer skin of the onion. On the cutting board, cut the onion in half. Place the halves flat side down on the cutting board and chop the onion.

2. Cut the tomato in half. Place the halves flat side down on the cutting board and slice the tomato. Cut each slice into small pieces. Set aside.

3. Heat the frying pan over medium heat and add the olive oil. Add the onion and cook for about 3 minutes until the onion is translucent.

4. Add the ground meat or poultry. With a wooden spoon, stir it around as it cooks, to break up any large clumps. Cook the meat until it is browned.

5. Place the colander in the sink and carefully pour the meat into it and allow the fat to drain.

6. Place the meat in the heatproof bowl. Mix the chili powder, cumin, and dried parsley into the meat.

7. If you wish to heat up the flat tortillas, place them on a microwave plate and cover with a paper towel. Microwave on high for 20 seconds.

8. Fill each tortilla or taco shell with 2 tablespoons of the meat mixture. Top as desired with lettuce, tomato, shredded cheese, and taco sauce. Serve immediately.

Ralph's Rib-Stickin' Hot and Spicy Texas Ribs

Time
1 hour

Tools
paper towels

liquid and dry measuring cups

measuring spoons

large pot or Dutch oven

tongs

medium bowl

wire whip

broiler pan

aluminum foil

oven mitts

pastry brush

Makes
4 servings

Barbecues and beef are a very important part of Texan cooking. Grilling foods over an open fire, hot stones, or coals, was a tradition carried on from the Native Americans. Ribs are a favorite Texas barbecue food. You can try this recipe outdoors on a grill or cook it indoors using a broiler.

Ingredients

12 spareribs

½ teaspoon salt

1 cup ketchup

1 tablespoon Worcestershire sauce

½ cup firmly packed brown sugar

½ tablespoon vinegar

1 tablespoon creamy mustard

½ teaspoon cumin

½ teaspoon chili powder

¼ teaspoon garlic salt

⅛ teaspoon cayenne pepper

2 drops Tabasco sauce

vegetable oil cooking spray

Steps

1. Wash the spare ribs with cool water and pat dry with paper towels.

2. Fill the large pot or Dutch oven with water. Add the salt and place over high heat. Once the water boils, place the spareribs in the water and reduce the heat so the water simmers. Simmer, uncovered, for about 45 minutes until the spareribs are tender. Using tongs set the spareribs on a plate to cool.

3. In the medium bowl, whisk together the ketchup, Worcestershire sauce, brown sugar, vinegar, mustard, cumin, chili powder, garlic salt, cayenne powder, and Tabasco sauce. Set aside.

4. If broiling indoors, preheat the broiler with the rack set 6 inches (15 cm) away from the broiling element. (If grilling outdoors, skip to step 9.)

5. Line the broiler pan with aluminum foil. Spray the foil lightly with vegetable oil cooking spray. Arrange the ribs in the lined pan.

6. Place the ribs under the broiler for 3 minutes. Keep your eyes on the ribs. Remove the pan with oven mitts.

7. Using tongs, turn the ribs over. Repeat the cooking on the other side of the ribs. Do not leave the broiler!

8. Using the pastry brush, brush the spicy sauce on one side of the ribs. Place under the broiler for 2 to 3 minutes and remove with the oven mitts. Turn the ribs over with the tongs and brush the other side with more spicy sauce. Place second side under the broiler for 3 minutes. Remove from the broiler with oven mitts and serve immediately.

9. If grilling outside, grill 4 inches from medium-hot coals for about 30 minutes. Turn frequently and brush sauce over the meat.

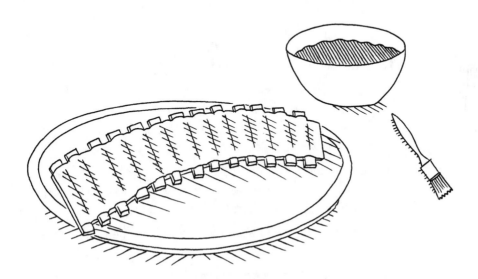

Time
1 hour 15 minutes

Tools
cutting board

paring knife

dry and liquid
measuring cups

measuring spoons

2 small bowls

large pot or
Dutch oven

wooden spoon

can opener

colander

zipper-lock
plastic bag

Makes
8 servings

Although chili sounds like it might have Mexican or Spanish roots, it really owes more to the Native Americans. Native Americans in the region used chili peppers long before Spanish or American settlers appeared.

Ingredients

2   green bell peppers

2   medium onions

2   cloves garlic

¼ cup olive oil

1   28-ounce can crushed tomatoes

2   tablespoons chili powder

1   tablespoon cumin

1   teaspoon dried parsley

1   teaspoon dried dill

1   teaspoon dried oregano

1   teaspoon dried basil

1   15-ounce can red kidney beans

1½ cups canned pinto beans

1   4-ounce can green chili peppers, mild

1   lemon

salt and pepper as needed

1   cup shredded cheddar cheese

Steps

1. Wash the bell peppers and pat dry.

2. On the cutting board, cut the tops off the peppers. Remove the seeds and discard. Cut the peppers in half and cut out the white ribs on the inside of the peppers. Dice the peppers into ¼-inch pieces.

3. Remove the thin papery skin from the onions. Cut the onions in half. Place the onion halves cut side down on the cutting board and chop into small pieces.

4. Remove the papery skin from the garlic. Then, mince the garlic.

5. Place the bell peppers, onions, and garlic in a small bowl and set aside.

6. Preheat the large pot or Dutch oven for 2 minutes on medium heat. Add the olive oil. Add the bell peppers, onion, and garlic and sauté for 10 minutes, stirring with a wooden spoon until softened and translucent.

7. Turn the heat to low, and add the crushed tomatoes, chili powder, cumin, parsley, dill, oregano, and basil. Cook uncovered for 30 minutes.

8. Drain the kidney beans, pinto beans, and chili peppers by placing them in a colander, and allowing the liquids to run through. Do not rinse.

9. Roll the lemon back and forth on the table about 5 or 6 times to loosen the membranes. Cut the lemon in half. Place one half in the plastic bag and refrigerate for another recipe. Squeeze the other half of the lemon over a small bowl to get 2 tablespoons of juice.

10. Stir the lemon juice, kidney beans, pinto beans, and chili peppers into the pot and cook for an additional 20 minutes.

11. Add salt and pepper as needed and mix well.

12. Serve the chili immediately and top with shredded cheddar cheese.

 PIONEER BREAKFAST

By 1840, much of the land between the Appalachian Mountains and the Mississippi River was settled, so the western frontier moved farther west into the plains and across the Rocky Mountains to the Pacific Ocean. The biggest phase of westward expansion took place from 1850 to 1900. One reason for this expansion was the discovery of gold in the mountains east of San Francisco in 1848. Gold was also found in Nevada, Colorado, Montana, Idaho, Arizona, and South

Dakota. The discovery of gold, as well as silver and copper, set many men and some women heading west hoping to find a fortune. Another reason settlers also moved west was to find inexpensive or even free land. The Homestead Act of 1862 gave settlers 160 acres of free land in the West if they lived on the land for five years and improved it. The early frontier settlers became known as pioneers.

The pioneers' journey west was long and hard. They loaded all their possessions into wagons and followed trails such as the Oregon Trail or the Santa Fe Trail. Families would stop wherever they found a good place to settle and begin building homes and clearing the land for farming. They would live in temporary shelters while they made homes out of logs or sod (hard, thick chunks of soil).

The number of settlers flooding into the West and claiming the land angered the Native Americans who had lived on these lands for years. Many battles broke out and the government forced many Native Americans to relocate far from their homes. The pioneers often lived in fear of raids and built forts and stockades to use in case of attacks.

The pioneers who settled on the prairie grew corns, beans, potatoes, squash, and other vegetables. Some vegetables, such as potatoes and beans, were kept during the winter in a pit dug in the ground that was called a **root cellar.** The vegetables did not freeze because they were kept below where the ground froze, and they stayed warmer.

Many pioneers hunted deer, wild turkeys, buffalo, and other wild animals. They also raised hogs, sheep, and chickens, and they may have kept a cow for milking. To keep fresh meat from spoiling, strips of meat were dried in the sun, smoked over a fire, or soaked in salt. For sweetness, pioneers used honey, maple syrup, and molasses.

FUN FOOD FACTS

- One pioneer meal was much like the next meal. Foods served for breakfast were likely to be served again for supper. It was not until the late 1800s that people associated certain foods with different meals, such as oatmeal for breakfast.

- Pioneers often did all their cooking using only three different types of pots: a frying pan, a tea kettle, and a Dutch oven (a kettle with a lid used for baking).

- Pioneers took advantage of the rough trails to churn milk into butter! The tossing of the wagon was often enough to shake the milk up enough to produce butter.

In the summer, the pioneers cooked outside over an open fire. On rainy days and in the winter, the fireplace was used to cook. Frontier food was simple and hearty. Stew was a common meal that was easy to make in a kettle hung over the fire. The kettle would be filled with some water; then strips of meat and whatever vegetables were available were added. Herbs, such as parsley, were picked and used to flavor foods. Corn kernels were ground into cornmeal, which was used to make different types of corn bread, such as **corn dodgers.** Corn dodgers were small cakes usually fried hard.

Buckwheat Griddle Cakes

Until the end of the 1800s, wheat was much more expensive than corn, rye, or buckwheat. Therefore, pancakes were often made out of cornmeal or buckwheat flour. **Buckwheat** is a plant that produces a triangle-shaped seed. Like wheat, buckwheat can be ground into a flour. Buckwheat has a stronger flavor than wheat flour. This recipe uses regular flour (from wheat) and buckwheat or whole wheat flour.

Time
20 minutes

Tools
dry and liquid
measuring cups
measuring spoons
medium bowl
small bowl
wire whip
wooden spoon
frying pan or griddle
ladle
spatula

Makes
16 4-inch pancakes

Ingredients

1 cup buckwheat flour or whole wheat flour

1 cup all-purpose flour

1 tablespoon baking powder

½ teaspoon salt

½ teaspoon ground cinnamon

¼ teaspoon ground nutmeg

2 eggs

1⅔ cup low-fat or skim milk

½ cup honey

¼ cup canola oil

1 teaspoon vanilla extract

vegetable oil cooking spray

Steps

1. Mix the flours, baking powder, salt, cinnamon, and nutmeg in the medium bowl. These are the dry ingredients.

2. Crack the eggs into the small bowl and beat lightly with the wire whip.

3. Add the eggs, milk, honey, canola oil, and vanilla extract to the dry ingredients. Stir with a wooden spoon just until blended.

4. Spray the frying pan or griddle with vegetable oil cooking spray.

5. Heat the frying pan or griddle over medium heat.

6. Ladle enough batter onto the griddle to make a 4-inch pancake. Cook until bubbles appear and the pancake is golden underneath.

7. Carefully turn the pancake with the spatula. Cook the other side until golden brown, about 1 minute.

8. Serve with maple syrup or your favorite jelly.

Amazing Country Scrambled Eggs

Breakfast was a big meal during pioneer times, including pancakes, eggs, sausages, fried potatoes, and more. Certainly the pioneers needed a big breakfast to do all the work that had to be done!

Time
30 minutes

Tools
dry and liquid measuring cups
measuring spoons
cutting board
paring knife
small bowl
wire whip
10-inch skillet
wooden spoon

Makes
4 servings

Ingredients

1 onion
1 green pepper
1 red pepper
8 eggs
¼ cup low-fat or skim milk
½ teaspoon salt

¼ teaspoon pepper
¼ teaspoon dried thyme
1 tablespoon olive oil
2 cups frozen diced potatoes, thawed
¾ cup shredded cheddar cheese

Steps

1. Remove the papery skin from the onion. On a cutting board, cut the onion in half and chop into small pieces.

2. Cut the green pepper in half lengthwise. With the knife, remove the seeds and the ribs. Cut each half into long strips, then chop into small pieces. Repeat the process with the red pepper.

3. In the small bowl, whisk together the eggs, milk, salt, pepper, and thyme.

4. Preheat the skillet over medium heat. Add the olive oil. Add the potatoes and onions to the skillet. Stir with a wooden spoon. Cook for about 5 minutes until the potatoes are lightly browned and the onions are soft and translucent.

5. Add the green and red peppers and cook for 3 more minutes.

6. Pour the egg mixture over the vegetables and gently stir for 4 to 5 minutes until the eggs are set.

7. Turn off the heat. Sprinkle cheese over the eggs and let sit for 2 minutes to melt the cheese before serving.

···· Trail Blazin' Beef Jerky ····

Beef jerky, or dried strips of beef, was a convenient food for pioneers. Since fresh beef could not be kept cold, it would go bad very quickly unless it was dried in the sun into jerky. This recipe shows how to make beef jerky with the help of an oven for drying.

Ingredients

3-pound London broil steak
1   teaspoon kosher salt
½ teaspoon pepper

1   cup soy sauce
vegetable oil cooking spray

Steps

1. On the cutting board with the help of a grown-up, cut the steak in half with the chef's knife. Cut each half into thin strips with the grain of the meat. Cutting with the grain means you will cut along the muscle fiber. If you cut against the muscle fiber the cooked meat will fall apart into small pieces!

2. Place the strips in the bowl and sprinkle with the salt and pepper. Add the soy sauce. Allow the strips to marinate for 30 minutes.

3. Meanwhile, preheat the oven to 170°F.

4. Cover the baking sheet with aluminum foil. Spray the foil lightly with vegetable oil cooking spray.

5. Remove the strips from the marinade and place in a single layer on the baking sheet. Discard the marinade.

6. Cook the beef jerky for 8½ hours until dry.

7. Use oven mitts to remove the baking sheet from the oven and store the beef in an airtight container.

Time
45 minutes to make
plus
8½ hours to cook
and dry out

Tools
liquid measuring cup
measuring spoons
cutting board
chef's knife
medium bowl
baking sheet
aluminum foil
oven mitts
airtight container

Makes
About 30 strips

CHAPTER 6

PLANTATION LIFE

In southern states where the soil and climate were excellent for farming, large farms called plantations prospered during the late eighteenth and early nineteenth centuries. Plantations were designed to produce large amounts of a single crop for export. Some plantation owners grew food crops, such as rice and sugar, but many grew tobacco and cotton because these products sold for more money. African slaves did virtually all the work on the plantation, in the fields, in the outbuildings, and in the main house, often known as the "Big House."

By 1860, over 800,000 slaves were living on plantations. Although some slaves lived in the owner's home or in a small building next to the owner's home, most lived in small cabins grouped together away from the owner's home. Many cabins had gardens where slaves grew crops to supplement the food given to them by the owner. Some slaves also had chickens.

Most slaves worked in the fields and in the plantation's work yard. Buildings surrounding the work yard typically included a well, a kitchen, a dairy, an icehouse, a chicken coop, a blacksmith, a laundry, a grist mill, and a smokehouse for smoking and storing meats. (Smoking was a process that preserved the meat.) A large plantation was really like a small town.

A few slaves worked in the Big House where they had many chores. They washed and ironed; spun, wove, and sewed clothing; tended gardens; cleaned the house; preserved foods; cooked meals; and took care of the owner's children.

Unlike northern homes in which the kitchen was inside the house, in southern plantations the kitchen was usually in a separate building to keep the heat, noise, and odors away from the main house.

Slaves did most of the cooking for the plantation family. Meats were baked, fried in lard (fat from pigs), or boiled. Slaves fried everything from chicken to catfish to the corn fritters called hush puppies. Their fondness for frying probably came from West Africa where foods were often fried in palm oil. Cooks used sweet spices such as cinnamon, nutmeg, and ginger to flavor baked foods such as cakes, pies, and cookies. Ingredients used in plantation cooking were influenced by Native Americans (corn, squash, beans, and nuts), Europeans (meat, eggs, and lard), and Africans (rice, black-eyed peas, and various green vegetables). Pecans, a locally grown nut, were harvested from trees in the fall, and used in a variety of dishes, such as pecan pie.

FUN FOOD FACTS

- Refrigerators were yet to be invented, so every plantation had an **icehouse**—a room built deep into the ground that was cool and could maintain ice from its frozen state. Slaves would cut the ice from frozen ponds during the winter and store it in the icehouse. On some plantations, ice was used to make ice cream.

- Confederate soldiers dined on peanut porridge—a soup made with peanuts, a popular southern ingredient. When Africans were brought to America as slaves, peanuts came with them. Slaves planted peanuts throughout the southern United States. Goober, the nickname for peanuts, comes from the Congo name for peanut: *nguba*.

In their slave quarters, slaves cooked the foods the master gave them every week, plus any vegetables and fruits they picked from their gardens or in the countryside, and, if they were allowed to hunt, game and fish. The slaves were not given much, so they did not waste any food. They ate parts of a hog that the master's family didn't want, and fish, such as catfish and perch, that no one else would eat. They used wild game in stews and gumbos. Even green tomatoes were fried or turned into pickles or pies.

Plantation life eventually disappeared after the Civil War between the Union states in the North and the Confederate states in the South, which took place from 1861 to 1865. Slavery had already been outlawed in the North, but was seen as a "necessary evil" to most people in the South. They couldn't imagine giving up their way of life completely by allowing all of their slaves to go free. When the Union won the war, Congress passed the Thirteenth Amendment to the Constitution, which outlawed slavery. Many soldiers from both sides died in the Civil War, and when it was over much of the South lay in ruins. The period after the Civil War is called **Reconstruction** because so much of the country had to be rebuilt.

Southern Fried Chicken Wings

Southern cooks prided themselves on preparing delicious, golden fried chicken. Here is an updated version that bakes the chicken, which is easier and healthier, but holds on to some of that deep-fried taste.

Ingredients

8 large chicken wings

1 cup all-purpose flour

½ teaspoon salt

⅛ teaspoon cayenne pepper

½ teaspoon thyme

¼ teaspoon tarragon

2 eggs

1 cup low-fat or skim milk

14 flavored crackers, such as Ritz

¼ cup yellow cornmeal

vegetable oil cooking spray

Steps

1. Preheat the oven to 400°F.

2. On the cutting board with the chef's knife, have an adult cut the chicken wings in half at the joint. Cut the wing tips off and discard. Be sure to wash the cutting board and the knife in very hot soapy water before putting away. Place the chicken wings on a tray.

3. In the medium bowl, mix together the flour, salt, cayenne pepper, thyme, and tarragon with a wooden spoon.

4. In the small bowl, whisk together the eggs and milk.

5. Place the flavored crackers in the plastic bag and seal, pressing all of the air out of the bag. Crush the crackers with a rolling pin using a back and forth motion, until the crackers break into fine crumbs. Add the cornmeal to the bag and mix with the cracker crumbs.

6. Cover the baking sheet with aluminum foil. Spray the foil with vegetable oil cooking spray.

7. Dredge the chicken wings in the flour mixture.

Time

20 minutes to prepare
plus
35 to 40
minutes to bake

Tools

dry and liquid
measuring cups

measuring spoons

cutting board

chef's knife

medium bowl

wooden spoon

small bowl

wire whip

large zipper-lock
plastic bag

rolling pin

baking sheet

aluminum foil

table fork

oven mitts

Makes

4 servings

8. Dip each wing in the egg and milk mixture, then put them in the cornmeal and cracker mixture and shake the bag until the wings are are completely covered.

9. Place on the baking sheet about 2 inches apart.

10. Bake the chicken for 35 to 40 minutes or until a fork inserted into the biggest wing shows clear juices. Take the baking sheet out of the oven with oven mitts and allow the chicken to rest for 10 minutes before serving.

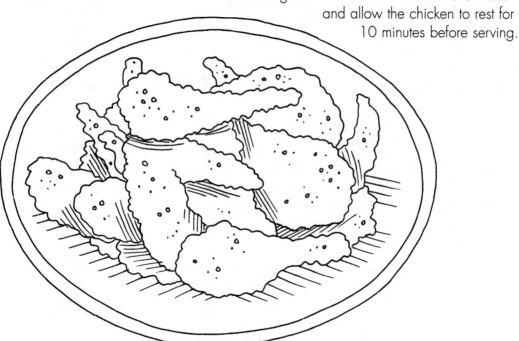

···· Plantation-Baked ····
Corn Bread

*Corn bread for the plantation family was baked in an oven, but the slaves sometimes baked their own corn bread right on the flat metal part of their hoes over a fire. These came to be known as **hoecakes** and were more like cornmeal pancakes.*

Ingredients

2   teaspoons vegetable shortening

1   cup all-purpose flour

1   cup yellow cornmeal

¼ cup sugar

1   tablespoon baking powder

½ teaspoon salt

⅛ teaspoon black pepper

1   cup low-fat or skim milk

¼ cup vegetable oil

¼ cup honey

2   large eggs, slightly beaten

1   cup frozen corn, thawed (optional)

Steps

1. Preheat the oven to 400°F.

2. Use the paper towel to grease the baking pan with the shortening.

3. In a medium bowl, mix together the flour and cornmeal with a wooden spoon. Stir well to combine. Add the sugar, baking powder, salt, and pepper and stir again.

4. In the other medium bowl, whisk together the milk, vegetable oil, honey, and eggs.

5. Add the milk mixture to the dry ingredients and stir just until the dry ingredients are moistened.

6. If you are using corn, fold it into the batter with a rubber spatula.

7. Pour the batter into the greased baking pan.

8. Bake for 20 to 25 minutes or until the bread is a light golden brown. Use oven mitts to remove from the oven.

Time
20 minutes to prepare
plus
20 to 25
minutes to bake

Tools
dry and liquid
measuring cups

measuring spoons

9-inch square
baking pan

paper towel

2 medium bowls

wooden spoon

wire whip

rubber spatula

oven mits

Makes
16 servings

The Sweetest Sweet Potato Pie

Time
15 minutes to prepare
plus
50 to 55
minutes to bake

Tools
dry and liquid
measuring cups

measuring spoons

2 medium bowls

potato masher

wire whip

small bowl

wooden spoon

baking sheet

oven mitts

wire rack

Makes
8 servings

Although it is called a pie, this dish was not served as dessert, but as part of the main meal. The slaves brought with them from Africa many ways to cook sweet potatoes. Native Americans had already been eating sweet potatoes here for many years.

Ingredients

1   17-ounce can sweet potatoes
    or yams

½ cup packed light brown sugar

½ cup molasses

1   teaspoon ground cinnamon

½ teaspoon ground ginger

½ teaspoon ground nutmeg

¼ teaspoon salt

3   eggs

1   cup low-fat or skim milk

1   9-inch prepared graham
    cracker pie shell

Steps

1. Preheat the oven to 375°F.

2. In a medium bowl, mash the sweet potatoes with the potato masher until smooth. Set aside.

3. In the other medium bowl, whisk together the brown sugar, molasses, cinnamon, ginger, nutmeg, and salt.

4. In the small bowl, whisk the eggs and milk together until well combined.

5. Add the egg mixture and the brown sugar mixture to the sweet potatoes. Stir with a wooden spoon until smooth.

6. Pour the mixture into the pie shell.

7. Place the pie on the baking sheet. Bake for 50 to 55 minutes or until the center is custardlike and set.

8. Take the pie out of the oven with oven mitts. Cool the pie on the wire rack for 15 minutes before serving.

Peaches and Cream Ice Cream Sundae with Gingersnaps

The peach industry flourished between 1850 and 1870 in South Carolina and Georgia. Europeans had brought peaches to the United States during colonial times. Ice cream also goes back to colonial times. Both George Washington and Thomas Jefferson had their own ice cream machines.

Ingredients

10 gingersnaps

½ teaspoon ground cinnamon

1 cup whipping cream

1 10-ounce can sliced peaches

1 pint vanilla ice cream

Steps

1. Put the medium mixing bowl and the beaters from the electric mixer in the freezer.

2. Place the gingersnaps in the plastic bag and seal, pressing all the air out of the bag. Crush with a rolling pin until the cookies are fine and crumbly. Add the cinnamon to the crumbs. Seal the bag and shake to mix.

3. Remove the bowl from the freezer and put the cream into it.

4. With the mixer on high speed, beat the cream until stiff peaks form when the beaters are lifted. This takes about 2 to 3 minutes. Do not overbeat!

5. Drain the peaches in the colander.

6. Spoon a scoop of ice cream into each of the serving cups or parfait glasses. Top with ⅛ of the peaches.

Time
20 minutes

Tools
medium mixing bowl
hand-held electric mixer with beaters
zipper-lock plastic bag
rolling pin
colander
ice cream scoop
liquid measuring cup
measuring spoons
4 serving cups or parfait glasses

Makes
4 sundaes

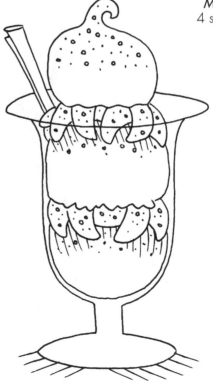

7. Sprinkle the ice cream and peaches with 2 teaspoons of the gingersnap crumbs.

8. Repeat steps 6 and 7, forming the second layer of the sundae.

9. Top the sundae with a dollop of the whipped cream and dust with the remaining gingersnaps crumbs.

CHAPTER 7

DINING ON THE TRANSCONTINENTAL RAILROAD

After the Civil War, even more Americans traveled west and settled down. Peace between the northern and southern states finally made it possible for a dream to be realized: the transcontinental railroad linking the Atlantic Coast to the Pacific Coast and cities to farms. In 1862, Congress granted two companies the right to build such a railroad. The Union Pacific started laying track in Omaha, Nebraska, heading west. The Central Pacific started laying track in Sacramento,

California, heading east. For every mile of track laid, the government granted railroads a certain amount of money and twenty square miles of land.

The two companies raced each other to earn money and land, but the work was brutal at times. There were tunnels to build through solid rock, blizzards and other bad weather to endure, dangerous chemicals to work with, and 500-pound rails to lift. In addition to employing many Americans, the railroads also employed thousands of Chinese, Irish, and other immigrant laborers. Seven years later, on May 10, 1869, the two tracks met and the last spike was driven with great ceremony in Promontory, Utah. Within twenty-five years, four more railroads crisscrossed the United States.

FUN FOOD FACTS

- The first refrigerator train cars used in the 1850s were simply wood cars containing ice. Companies used refrigerator cars to transport beef and other meats. Later on, the special cars transported fruits. The refrigerator cars were very important in improving the distribution of food.

- Many railroad companies were known for making certain regional dishes. For example, the Baltimore & Ohio was famous for its Chesapeake Bay seafood, while the Santa Fe was known for its broiled sage hen and prairie chicken. Most meals cost one dollar.

The first dining cars on the transcontinental railroad were for first-class passengers. George Pullman designed luxurious dining cars as well as sleeping cars. The first class passengers received superb meals including such foods as roast beef, antelope steaks, broiled chicken, fresh trout, corn on the cob, fresh fruit, hot rolls, corn bread, ice cream, and pies.

Dining cars for other passengers were not available until the late 1880s. Until then, most passengers took their meals at railroad stations. Food and service at railroad stations were terrible until the arrival of Frederick Harvey from London. In 1876 Harvey made a deal with the Santa Fe railroad to open a restaurant in Topeka, Kansas. The restaurant was clean, well run, and had excellent food at moderate prices. Cowboys had to remove their hats and put on a jacket to be served. The restaurant was an overnight success and eventually Harvey obtained the exclusive right to operate all restaurants along the Santa Fe line.

The only problem Harvey had with his restaurants was getting good waiters. The male waiters he hired were often trouble—they drank too much, they fought too much, and they didn't shave enough. To resolve this problem, he advertised in

the East for young women to work in his Harvey Houses. Once the women came, they were fitted for uniforms, given a room in the supervised dormitory, and trained for thirty days. They became known as the "Harvey Girls," and were highly regarded in the West.

Most Harvey Houses offered both "Lunch Room Service" (served at a lunch counter) and dining room service. The dining room menu was fancier and offered foods such as stuffed turkey with cranberry sauce, filet of whitefish with Madeira sauce, sugar-cured ham, boiled sweet potatoes, and mashed potatoes. The Lunch Room served less expensive foods, such as fried chicken with country gravy, minute sirloin steak with mushroom sauce, Hungarian goulash, filled omelets, minced brown potatoes, sliced tomatoes with French dressing, and pies, ice cream, and sherbet for dessert.

Chop Suey

Chop suey is an American dish that may have been created by Chinese cooks serving the men who built the transcontinental railroad. This main dish combines typical American ingredients of the time such as pork, with Chinese ingredients such as bean sprouts.

Time
35 minutes

Tools
paper towels
paring knife
cutting board
dry and liquid measuring cups
measuring spoons
wok or large frying pan with lid
wooden spoon
small bowl

Makes
6 servings

Ingredients

2 stalks celery

6 green onions (also called scallions)

2 cups sliced fresh mushrooms

1 pound boneless pork or boneless chicken breast

1 tablespoon vegetable oil

1 cup chicken broth

2 tablespoons soy sauce

2 tablespoons cornstarch

2 tablespoons cold water

1 8-ounce can sliced water chestnuts or bamboo shoots, drained

1 16-ounce can bean sprouts, drained and rinsed

3 cups cooked rice

Steps

1. Wash the celery, green onions, and mushrooms. Pat dry with paper towels.

2. Using the paring knife and cutting board, cut off the leaves and ends of the celery. Slice the celery diagonally into ¼-inch slices.

3. Cut off the roots and green leaf ends of the scallions. Cut the scallions into ¼-inch slices.

4. If using pork, trim off any fat. Slice the pork or chicken into thin, bite-size strips.

5. In the wok or large frying pan, heat the oil over medium-high heat. Add the pork or chicken and stir-fry for 3 to 4 minutes. When stir-frying, use the wooden spoon to keep the food moving around the wok so that it cooks evenly and does not burn.

6. Add the celery to the wok. Stir-fry for 2 minutes.

7. Add the scallions and mushrooms. Stir-fry for 2 minutes.

8. Add the chicken broth and soy sauce to the stir-fry. Bring to a boil by covering for about 2 minutes.

9. While waiting for the stir-fry to boil, mix the cornstarch and cold water in the small bowl until smooth.

10. Add the cornstarch mixture slowly to the stir-fry, stirring constantly. Cook the stir-fry until thickened and bubbly.

11. Add the water chestnuts and bean sprouts. Cook and stir till heated through.

12. Serve with cooked rice.

···· Coast-to-Coast ····
Apple Pie

Apple pie was a regular on the Harvey House menu, and was also served in the railroad dining car.

Ingredients

6 to 7 medium Delicious apples or other baking apples

¼ cup sugar

2 tablespoons all-purpose flour

½ teaspoon ground cinnamon

¼ teaspoon ground ginger

1 teaspoon vanilla extract

2 frozen 9-inch pie crusts

Steps

1. Preheat the oven to 375°F.

3. To make the pie filling, first wash and dry the apples. Peel the apples.

2. Use the apple corer to core the apples. Slice the apples on the cutting board into ¼-inch slices.

4. In the large bowl, combine the sugar, flour, cinnamon, and ginger. Stir in the apples and vanilla.

5. Put the filling into one of the pie crusts. Take the other crust and lay it over the top of the pie. Let thaw 10 minutes. Use your fingers to seal the edges of the two crusts together. Use a knife to make a few small slits in the top crust.

Time
40 minutes to prepare
plus
45 to 55
minutes to bake

Tools
peeler
apple corer
knife
cutting board
large bowl
dry measuring cup
measuring spoons
oven mitts
aluminum foil

Makes
9-inch pie, about
8 servings

6. Bake the pie for 25 minutes. Then, using oven mitts, loosely place a piece of aluminum foil around the edge of the pie so it doesn't get too brown. Bake 20 more minutes or until the top is golden and the fruit is bubbly.

Cocoanut Pudding

Menus from the fancy Pullman dining cars show a dessert by this name. Cocoanut is simply another way to spell coconut.

Ingredients

3 cups low-fat or skim milk

⅓ cup uncooked long-grain rice

¾ cup flaked coconut

¼ cup sugar

1 teaspoon vanilla extract

¼ teaspoon ground nutmeg

Steps

1. Put the milk in the saucepan, and place on a burner over medium heat. Bring the milk to a boil (look for bubbles, which means that it's starting to boil).

2. Stir in the rice with the wooden spoon.

3. Reduce the heat to low and cover the pan. Cook for 30 to 40 minutes or until most of the milk is absorbed.

4. Remove the pan from the heat. Stir in the coconut, sugar, and vanilla extract.

5. Pour the pudding in the bowl. Sprinkle with nutmeg and place in the refrigerator to cool.

Time
15 minutes to prepare
plus
30 to 40 minutes to cook

Tools
liquid and dry measuring cups

measuring spoons

2-quart saucepan with lid

wooden spoon

medium bowl

Makes
6 ½-cup servings

 VICTORIAN TEA

The Victorian Era in Britain and the United States was named after Queen Victoria of England who reigned from 1837 to 1901. During this period, England saw tremendous growth of its power and wealth. Both England and the United States entered the Industrial Revolution, a period when machines were developed to mass produce items and make workers more productive. Urban areas grew and suburbs appeared.

After the American Civil War, industries spread across the United States. By the end of the century, millions of Americans were working in huge factories. Many, including children, were working long hours for low pay, while a few bosses made huge fortunes. Eventually, workers started to organize **labor unions,** groups of workers who banded together to demand better pay and working conditions. At the same time, many women were banding together to demand the right to vote.

The late 1800s were also a time of amazing inventions. Americans invented the telephone, electric lighting, electric street-cars, the record player, and the movie camera. In 1896, Henry Ford built his first automobile. In the United States, middle-class life centered around the family and home. Favorite pastimes were reading, card playing, picnics, needlecrafts, singing, and lawn games such as croquet. Education was important, and free public education became more common after the Civil War.

Wealthy families lived in mansions, ate elaborate meals in elegant dining rooms, and visited with guests in fancy parlors. Dinner would often begin with oysters, then soup. The main course included dishes such as fillet of beef, lamb chops, creamed chicken, poached salmon, boiled potatoes, and asparagus. Dessert might have included molded ice cream, cakes, pies, and fruit, followed by coffee and tea. The meal was long and took lots of time to cook. These types of meals were only possible because of hired help including cooks, waiters, maids, and others. Dinner parties among the upper class were even longer, featuring twelve to eighteen courses.

During the period between 1880 and 1920, known as the Progressive Era, over 36 million people came to America. Over two and half million of the immigrants were Jews fleeing anti-Jewish violence. Cities grew bigger as immigrants and people from the country moved in. Immigrants often had a hard time finding housing, getting jobs, and fitting in due to their different languages, clothing, and foods. Many lived in small, crowded, dark tenement rooms that they could barely afford to rent. Italian spaghetti, Irish stew, and Hungarian goulash are examples of dishes added to America's kitchens during this period.

Late in the 1800s, foods in individual packages started to make appearances. Packaged foods such as Jell-O became available in sealed cardboard boxes. Foods were also packaged in glass bottles and tin cans. In a quest for healthier breakfast foods, John Harvey Kellogg invented wheat flakes. His brother, Will, invented Corn Flakes. C. W. Post soon introduced Grape-Nuts. Processed foods such as these changed breakfast for many Americans and also shortened the Victorian midday dinner. As Campbell's soup company told its customers, soup could be a meal in itself for lunch. Convenience foods also invaded suppertime. Canned spaghetti and meat stew did not need to be cooked, only reheated. Packaged cake mixes and puddings made desserts easy to prepare as well.

FUN FOOD FACTS

- During Victorian times, around the mid-1800s, stuffed turkey became the centerpiece of the American Christmas feast. It was often served with oyster dressing, cranberry sauce, sweet potatoes, mincemeat pie, oranges, and nuts.
- Puddings that were boiled or steamed were a great favorite in both England and the United States during the age of Victoria. Some used dried fruits such as figs.

Lemon and Poppy Seed Afternoon Tea Bread

Afternoon tea is a tradition begun by the English Duchess of Bedford in 1840. Wealthy Americans took to mimicking their British cousins by serving miniature sandwiches, fancy cakes, and pastries.

Ingredients

1 tablespoon shortening

3 cups plus 1 tablespoon all-purpose flour

½ teaspoon baking soda

1½ tablespoons poppy seeds

1 lemon

4 large eggs

2 cups sugar

1 cup low-fat or skim milk

½ cup (1 stick) margarine

Steps

1. Grease the loaf pan with a paper towel and shortening. Dust the pan with 1 tablespoon of flour by shaking the flour all over the pan. Make sure you work over the sink.

2. In a medium bowl, mix together 3 cups of flour, the baking soda, and the poppy seeds with the wooden spoon. Set aside.

3. Roll the lemon back and forth on a flat surface to loosen the inner membranes.

4. Using the peeler, peel the outer yellow skin off the lemon.

5. Place the lemon skin on a cutting board and chop into small pieces with a knife to make lemon zest. (You can also snip the lemon skin into very small pieces using a kitchen scissors).

6. Cut the lemon in half. Squeeze out 1 tablespoon of lemon juice and set it aside in a small cup. Discard the used lemon half. Wrap the other half and save it in the refrigerator.

7. In the other medium bowl, whisk together the eggs and sugar. Add the lemon zest pieces.

Time
20 minutes to prepare
plus
70 to 80
minutes to bake

Tools
dry and liquid measuring cups

measuring spoons

9 x 5-inch loaf pan

paper towel

2 medium bowls

wooden spoon

peeler

cutting board

kitchen scissors

paring knife

cup

wire whip

small bowl

small microwave dish

toothpick

oven mitts

wire rack

Makes
9-inch loaf, about 18 servings

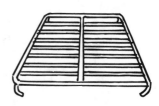

8. Put the lemon juice and milk together in the small bowl. Let it sit for 5 minutes to sour. Add the milk mixture to the eggs and sugar and mix well.

9. In a small microwave dish, melt the margarine on high power for about 30 seconds. Add the margarine to the milk mixture.

10. Combine the milk mixture and the flour mixture. Stir well with the wooden spoon just until all of the dry ingredients are moistened.

11. Pour the batter into the greased and floured pan.

12. Bake for 70 to 80 minutes until the top of the tea bread is golden brown and a toothpick inserted into the middle of the bread comes out clean.

13. Take the bread out of the oven with oven mitts.

14. Let the bread sit in the pan for 10 minutes and then turn onto a wire rack to completely cool.

Old-Fashioned Root Beer Float

Root beer was a very popular flavoring in the Victorian era for both candy and beverages. The ice cream float first appeared sometime in the late nineteenth century, but no one is sure who invented it.

Time
5 minutes

Tools
liquid measuring cup
4 tall glasses
ice cream scoop

Makes
4 floats

Ingredients

4   cups root beer soda

4   large scoops vanilla ice cream

Steps

1. Pour 1 cup of soda into each of 4 tall glasses.

2. Top each glass with a large scoop of vanilla ice cream and serve.

···· Noodle Kugel ····

Time
25 minutes to prepare, plus
1 hour for baking

Tools
large saucepan
wooden spoon
colander
microwave dish
large bowl
2 small bowls
fork
dry measuring cups
measuring spoons
13 × 9-inch baking dish
oven mitts

Makes
10 servings

During the Progressive era, many Jewish people immigrated to the United States from Europe. Kugel comes from a German word that has come to mean a baked casserole or pudding. Noodle kugel is a type of pudding made with noodles that is served with the main course or as dessert. Quite often, it is made with raisins or apples.

Ingredients

1 12-ounce package broad egg noodles

½ cup (1 stick) margarine

5 eggs

1 16-ounce container cottage cheese

1 16-ounce container sour cream

1¼ cups sugar

1 tablespoon vanilla extract

1 cup raisins or 2 large apples, peeled and chopped (optional)

1 teaspoon ground cinnamon

Steps

1. Fill the saucepan half full with water, place it over a high heat, and bring the water to a boil.

2. Gradually add the noodles to the boiling water. Stir gently with the wooden spoon.

3. Return to a rapid boil. Cook uncovered for 6 minutes. Stir occasionally.

4. Preheat the oven to 350°F.

5. Place the colander in the sink and drain the egg noodles.

6. Melt the margarine in the microwave at full power for 30 seconds or until it turns to a liquid. When the margarine is melted, pour it into the large bowl.

7. Crack the eggs into a small bowl and beat the eggs with a fork.

8. Add the eggs to the margarine and stir.

9. Add the cottage cheese, sour cream, 1 cup sugar, and the vanilla to the bowl with the eggs and margarine. Stir. If you are using apples or raisins stir them in.

10. Add the noodles to the bowl with the other ingredients. Stir well.

11. Spoon the mixture into the baking dish.

12. Stir together the cinnamon and $\frac{1}{4}$ cup sugar in a small bowl. Sprinkle the pudding with cinnamon sugar.

13. Bake for 1 hour.

14. Using oven mitts, remove from the oven and cool at least 10 minutes before cutting into squares. Serve warm.

CHAPTER 9

THE RAVENOUS ROARING TWENTIES

When World War I ended in 1918, America entered a period of peace and prosperity. During World War I, the United States joined Great Britain and France in successfully fighting against Germany and other countries called the "Central Powers." American soldiers, called **doughboys,** returned home victorious to an America bursting with energy and excitement.

During the 1920s, which became known as the "Roaring Twenties," business was booming. Radios, electricity, and cars became more affordable and much more common. The first commercial radio station began broadcasting in 1920 and there were more than 600 radio stations within ten years. Americans had shorter working hours and more time for leisure activities, such as listening to music and watching sports. Some of the well-known sports heroes of the time included baseball's Babe Ruth and Lou Gehrig, football's Red Grange, and boxing's Jack Dempsey. Americans listened to a new form of music invented by black musicians in the South called **jazz.** The 1920s were also known as the Jazz Age. The most well-known jazz band during the 1920s was King Oliver's Creole Jazz Band, which featured trumpeter Louis Armstrong. Young women began wearing dresses with low necklines and short hemlines. People danced wild new dances, such as the Charleston, and had dance marathons.

Not everyone shared in the wealth of the 1920s. Farmers and African Americans were among those untouched by the prosperity of the period. Farmers did well during World War I because crop prices were high. After the war, prices fell. African American farmers in the South often worked as **sharecroppers,** meaning that they farmed some land in exchange for giving the owner of the land a certain percentage of the crops. Sharecroppers barely made enough money to live on, if that much.

The 1920s are also known for **Prohibition.** Prohibition, which lasted from 1920 to 1933, was a period during which it was illegal to make or sell alcoholic beverages. No law has ever been so ignored. During the 1920s, Americans continued to drink at secret taverns called speakeasies, and began the tradition of having cocktail parties (parties with alcoholic drinks) at home. Cocktail parties inspired the development of finger foods, such as celery stuffed with cream cheese or blue cheese, seasoned tuna fish in tiny balls rolled in parsley, and **canapés** (open-face, bite-size sandwiches). Finger foods worked well for guests who had to juggle drinks, food, and cigarettes while walking around and chatting with others. The ban on liquor also created a new appetite for soft drinks, ice cream sodas, coffee, and candy bars.

At the beginning of the 1920s, most kitchens still used ice to keep foods cold and wood or coal in the stoves. During the 1920s, electric refrigerator sales jumped. Gas ranges started to replace wood and coal stoves. By 1930, the electric range arrived. Pop-up toasters and stainless steel knives were new to the market. Packaged bread that was presliced was sold for the first time during the 1920s. Popular recipes of the 1920s included Swiss steak, Italian spaghetti, chiffon pies, and salads, such as the Caesar, the Cobb, and the Golden Glow (carrots and pineapple in orange gelatin).

Also during the 1920s, Americans began to take a more scientific approach to food and nutrition. Home economists were busy developing recipes and menus that would ensure the physical and economic well-being of American families. Scientists were discovering vitamins, substances in food that are needed for growth and good health.

Many of the foods and recipes of the Roaring Twenties endure, but the "good life" came to an abrupt end with the stock market crash in 1929, the topic of the next chapter.

FUN FOOD FACTS

- All of the following candy bars came out in the 1920s: Baby Ruth, O'Henry, Mounds, Milky Way, Reese's Peanut Butter Cups, Mr. Goodbar, and Butterfinger.

- In 1927, Edwin Perkins modified his popular soft drink syrup, Fruit Smack, by concentrating it into a powder. He packaged it and changed the name to Kool-Ade. The name soon changed to Kool-Aid.

- The humble ice cream cone evolved into new products in the 1920s, including the Popsicle, the Good Humor Bar, and the Eskimo Pie.

Baby Ruth Homerun Bars

In the 1920s, Babe Ruth's star was rising as a baseball player for the Yankees. The Baby Ruth candy bar, developed in 1921, may or may not have been named for him. (Some say it was named after President Grover Cleveland's daughter, but she had died in 1904.) Whatever story you believe, these bars, made with Baby Ruth candy bars, are truly a "homerun."

Time
35 minutes to prepare
plus
30 minutes to bake

Tools
9 × 13-inch baking dish
dry measuring cups
measuring spoons
2 medium bowls
hand-held electric mixer
2 small bowls
table fork
wooden spoon
cutting board
paring knife
wire whip
oven mitts

Makes
24 bars

Ingredients

vegetable oil cooking spray
½ cup (1 stick) margarine
½ cup peanut butter
1 cup sugar
1 cup firmly packed brown sugar
2 eggs
2 teaspoons vanilla extract
2 Baby Ruth candy bars, or 4 Mini-Ruth bars

3 cups plus 1 tablespoon all-purpose flour
1 teaspoon baking soda
1 teaspoon salt
½ cup unsalted peanut halves
½ cup raisins
¼ cup chocolate chips

Steps

1. Preheat the oven to 375°F.

2. Spray the baking dish with vegetable oil cooking spray.

3. Place the margarine and peanut butter in a medium bowl.

4. With the electric mixer on medium speed, beat the margarine and peanut butter together for about 3 minutes until light and fluffy.

5. Add the sugar and brown sugar to the bowl. Continue beating until the sugars are combined with the margarine mixture.

6. Crack open the two eggs in a small bowl. Beat lightly with a fork.

7. Add the eggs and vanilla extract to the margarine mixture. Stir with the wooden spoon.

8. On a cutting board with a sharp knife, chop the Baby Ruth candy bars into small pieces. In the other small bowl, toss the candy pieces with 1 tablespoon of flour. Place the bowl in the refrigerator to firm up for 10 minutes.

9. In the other medium bowl, mix the baking soda, salt, and 3 cups of flour together with the wire whip.

10. Combine the flour mixture with the margarine mixture and stir.

11. Add the candy bar pieces, peanut halves, raisins, and chocolate chips. Stir just until all of the flour particles are moistened. You will have a soft dough. Place it in the refrigerator for 10 minutes to rest.

12. Turn the dough out of the bowl and press it into the baking dish with the heel of your hand.

13. Bake for 25 to 30 minutes or until bars are lightly golden brown and set in the middle. Remove from oven using oven mitts.

14. Allow the bars to sit for 20 minutes in the pan before cutting into squares.

•••• Fast 'n' Easy Caesar Salad ••••

During Prohibition, stars from Hollywood, California, would travel down to Mexico to go to restaurants that served alcohol. Caesar Cardini owned one such restaurant in Tijuana, Mexico, in 1924. One busy weekend when he was running low on food, he created a salad using romaine lettuce, oil, eggs, lemon juice, Worcestershire sauce, salt, and pepper. The salad was a hit, and became known as Caesar salad. This fast and easy recipe uses a premade Caesar salad dressing.

Time
10 minutes

Tools
paring knife

cutting board

large wooden salad bowl

paper towels

dry and liquid measuring cups

wooden spoon

Makes
6 servings

Ingredients

1 clove garlic

1 large head romaine lettuce

1 cup bottled Caesar salad dressing

¼ cup grated Parmesan or Romano cheese

1½ cups croutons

Steps

1. Peel the outer skin from the clove of garlic. Using a paring knife, cut the clove in half lengthwise.

2. Rub the inside of the salad bowl with the garlic, then discard the garlic.

3. Wash the lettuce under cold, running water. Pat dry with paper towels.

4. Break the lettuce into bite-size pieces and put into the salad bowl.

5. Add the salad dressing and grated cheese and toss with the wooden spoon.

6. Top the salad with the croutons and serve.

•••••••• •••• Supremely Citrus Sundae •••• •••••••••

Time
30 minutes to
prepare gelatin
plus
4 hours to set
plus
15 minutes to assemble

Tools
liquid measuring cup

2-quart saucepan

3 medium heatproof
bowls

wooden spoon

medium mixer bowl

handheld electric
mixer

grater

cutting board

paring knife

4 tall glasses or 8-ounce
clear tumblers

Makes
4 servings

In the 1920s, sales of Jell-O grew as more and more homes included refrigerators. Jell-O had been around since the 1800s, but lack of refrigeration made the product less desirable then.

Ingredients

6   cups water

1   3-ounce package orange Jell-O

1   3-ounce package lemon Jell-O

1   3-ounce package lime Jell-O

1   cup whipping cream

2   limes

Steps

1. Place 1 cup of water in the saucepan.

2. Open the package of orange gelatin, and put the contents into a heatproof bowl.

3. Place the saucepan over medium heat, and bring the water to a boil.

4. Carefully pour the boiling water into the bowl with the orange gelatin. Stir the gelatin with a wooden spoon for at least 2 minutes until it completely dissolves.

5. Add 1 cup of cold water to the gelatin mixture and stir for 2 minutes.

6. Refrigerate the gelatin, uncovered, for about 4 hours or until firm.

7. Repeat steps 1 through 6 using the lemon and then the lime Jell-O.

8. Once the gelatin is firm, pour the cream into the medium mixer bowl.

9. Using the hand-held electric mixer, beat the cream until stiff peaks form. Set aside in the refrigerator while you prepare the limes.

10. Rub the skin of 1 lime across the grater's tiny holes to make lime zest. Be careful not to include any of the white pith when you are grating. You will have about 1 tablespoon when you are done.

11. Cut the second lime into slices on the cutting board.

12. To assemble the dessert, place about one quarter of the orange gelatin in a clear tall glass or tumbler. Repeat with the lemon and lime gelatin.

13. Place a dollop of whipped cream on the top of the gelatin.

14. Sprinkle the whipped cream with the lime zest. Garnish the side of the glass with a slice of lime. Make 3 more desserts and serve.

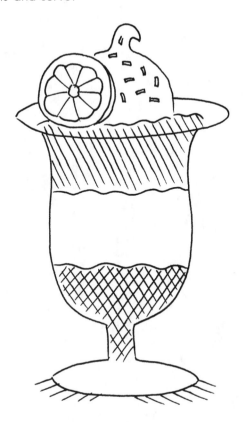

CHAPTER 10

MAKING DO DURING THE GREAT DEPRESSION

The 1930s were known as the decade of the **Great Depression.** The hard times came to the United States in late 1929 with the collapse of the stock market. Many people had borrowed huge amounts of money in the 1920s to buy stocks, new cars, clothes, and household goods. As people's debts grew, they stopped buying new products. As spending went down, businesses lost money and the value of their stocks went down. Workers were laid off from their jobs. Farmers were also in bad shape from years of getting low prices for their crops.

Then, on October 29, 1929, the stock market "crashed," meaning that stock prices dropped to very, very low levels. Millions of people who had purchased stocks lost everything. Because loans were not being paid back, banks failed and could not give money to people who had deposited money. Many people lost their entire savings. Factories, stores, and mines closed down due to lack of money. People who had never been out of work were without jobs and living in poverty. Some Americans who had lost their homes were forced to build temporary shacks to live in. These towns became known as "Hoovervilles" because the residents blamed President Herbert Hoover for the Great Depression. By 1932, at the lowest point of the Depression, almost 12 million Americans were unemployed.

In 1933, a new president, Franklin Delano Roosevelt, took over. Roosevelt believed strongly in spending government money to help the poor. Roosevelt talked to the American people on the radio to lift people's spirits, and he promised action to get the country turned around. He put together a large number of new government programs, called the "New Deal," to get people back to work, money back in the banks, and businesses back on their feet. By 1940, the economy was better.

During the Depression years, people made the best of what little they had and tried to forget their troubles by listening to the radio and going to the movies. The 1930s are remembered as the golden age of radio and movies. Radio shows included the Lone Ranger, Superman, and Dick Tracy. At age six, Shirley Temple started her acting career and became a popular movie star. In 1939, *The Wizard of Oz* was released.

Heroes from the 1930s include Jesse Owens and Amelia Earhart. Jesse Owens was an African American track-and-field athlete who set three world records and won four gold medals at the 1936 Olympic Games in Nazi Germany. Amelia Earhart was the first woman to fly across the Atlantic Ocean to Europe

FUN FOOD FACTS

- During the 1930s, Girl Scouts in Philadelphia started selling cookies to raise money for summer camp. The idea became popular in more Girl Scout troops and soon commercial bakers were asked to make Girl Scout shortbread cookies that were sold across the United States.

- In 1934, Ritz crackers were created. The name was meant to make people think of Manhattan's luxurious Ritz-Carlton Hotel. The crackers were rich and buttery, but very affordable at nineteen cents a box.

- In 1930, Twinkies were created by a Hostess plant manager.

by herself. She was mourned in 1937 when her plane was lost while she was trying to fly around the world.

Home cooks relied on women's magazines, radio shows, and cookbooks like *The Joy of Cooking* for tips on how to make meals on a limited budget. Many recipes of the era used little or no meat because meat was expensive and hard to get. Chili, macaroni and cheese, meat loaf, spaghetti with meatballs, creamed chicken on biscuits, and soups were popular. Sugar prices were low, so home cooks made lots of sweet desserts. For people who were less fortunate, soup kitchens run by different charities offered free meals of bread with soups, stews, and other hot foods.

Speedy Vegetable and Barley Soup

Hearty vegetable soups, such as this one, provided good nutrition to the people on the soup lines.

Ingredients

1   clove garlic
1   onion
2   large carrots
¼ head cabbage
2   tablespoons olive oil
6   cups vegetable stock or broth
¼ cup barley

2   cups tomato purée
2   cups frozen cubed turnips, thawed
1   teaspoon dried oregano
1   teaspoon dried basil
10-ounce package frozen mixed vegetables, thawed
salt and pepper as needed

Time
60 minutes

Tools
dry and liquid measuring cups
measuring spoons
cutting board
paring knife
vegetable peeler
large pot or Dutch oven
wooden spoon

Makes
8 1-cup servings

Steps

1. Remove the papery skin from the garlic clove. On the cutting board with a sharp knife, mince the garlic.

2. Remove the papery outer skin from the onion. Cut the onion in half. Put the halves flat side down on the cutting board and chop into large pieces.

3. Using a peeler, peel the outer skin off the carrots. Slice each carrot into ¼-inch slices.

4. Place the cabbage flat side down on the cutting board and cut into shreds.

5. Preheat the large pot or Dutch oven on medium heat for 2 minutes.

6. Add the olive oil to the pot. Sauté the garlic and the onions together for about 2 minutes, stirring with the wooden spoon until the onion is clear and the garlic is light golden brown.

7. Add the vegetable stock and barley to the pot. Bring to a boil, then lower the heat and simmer, uncovered, for 40 minutes.

8. Add the tomato purée, turnips, carrots, cabbage, oregano, and basil to the pot and continue to cook for 30 minutes more.

9. Stir in the mixed vegetables and season with salt and pepper. Cook 10 more minutes until all of the vegetables are tender.

10. Serve in soup bowls.

Baked Macaroni and Cheese

This dish was popular during the Depression (and still is today) because it was tasty and inexpensive.

Ingredients

4 quarts water

1 pound elbow macaroni

4 cups skim or low-fat milk

2 cups evaporated skim milk

4 tablespoons (½ stick) margarine

½ cup all-purpose flour

3 cups grated sharp cheddar cheese

1½ cups grated Swiss cheese

3 tablespoons unflavored bread crumbs

Time
40 minutes to prepare
plus
25 minutes to bake

Tools
2 large saucepans
wooden spoon
colander
casserole dish
medium saucepan

Makes
8 servings

Steps

1. Bring the water to a boil in a large saucepan.

2. Add the macaroni in batches, stirring after each addition with the wooden spoon.

3. Cook the macaroni for about 8 minutes or until almost tender.

4. Place the colander in the sink and drain the macaroni. Transfer the macaroni to the casserole dish.

5. Preheat the oven to 350°F.

6. Put the skim milk and evaporated milk in the medium saucepan and place on a burner over medium-high heat. Bring the milk just to a boil, then turn off the heat and remove from the burner.

7. Melt the margarine in a large saucepan over low heat. Cook until it's a little bubbly.

8. Add the flour to the margarine, and cook for 4 minutes over low heat, stirring frequently with a wooden spoon.

9. Slowly add the hot milk to the flour mixture, stirring constantly over low heat, until all the milk has been added.

10. Add the cheeses to the saucepan and cook until the cheese has melted.

11. Pour the cheese sauce over the macaroni, then sprinkle with bread crumbs.

12. Bake for 25 minutes until golden brown.

Depression Cake

Depression era cooks made cakes that omitted expensive ingredients such as butter, milk, and eggs. This recipe uses sugar, but it has no eggs, butter, or milk.

Ingredients

1 cup shortening

2 cups water

2 cups raisins

1 teaspoon ground cinnamon

1 teaspoon ground nutmeg

1 teaspoon ground allspice

½ teaspoon ground cloves

2 cups sugar

vegetable oil cooking spray

3 cups all-purpose flour

1 teaspoon baking soda

Steps

1. In the saucepan, combine the shortening, water, raisins, cinnamon, nutmeg, allspice, cloves, and sugar.

2. Simmer the mixture over medium heat for 10 minutes. Remove from heat and cool for 10 minutes.

3. Preheat the oven to 350°F.

4. Spray the baking pan with vegetable oil cooking spray.

5. Sift the flour and baking soda into the cooled raisin mixture. Mix with a wooden spoon until just combined.

6. Pour the batter into the baking pan.

7. Bake for 45 minutes.

8. Using oven mitts, remove the cake from the oven and cool on the wire rack.

Time
25 minutes to prepare
plus
45 minutes to bake

Tools
large saucepan

dry and liquid measuring cups

measuring spoons

wooden spoon

9 x 13-inch baking pan

sifter

oven mitts

wire rack

Makes
24 servings

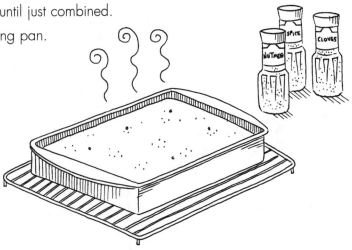

CHAPTER 11

ORLD WAR II RATIONS

In 1939, World War II began when Adolf Hitler invaded Poland. Hitler joined with the dictators of Japan and Italy, and together they planned to conquer the world. France and England declared war on Germany. The United States stayed out of the war until 1941 when the Japanese bombed Pearl Harbor, a naval base in Hawaii, destroying eighteen ships and killing over two thousand Americans. The United States could no longer remain isolated from the rest of the world, and declared war on Japan, Germany, and Italy. Hundreds of thousands of

American soldiers went off to fight in Europe, Africa, and the South Pacific.

While American soldiers were making sacrifices on the war front, Americans at home were asked to make sacrifices, too. To replace the men who left to fight, women went to work in factories, making tanks, machine guns, jeeps, and just about anything else needed for war. Americans at home were asked to "Do with Less—So the Soldiers Will Have Enough." The war required many ships, aircraft, tanks, and weapons, and huge amounts of munitions and other supplies. Children saved metal, paper, and rubber and took them to scrap drives so they could be used to make goods for war.

Many food items like meat and cheese became scarce because soldiers needed them overseas. The government issued food ration stamps to make sure these foods were distributed fairly. First sugar and coffee were rationed, then meat, butter, margarine, cheese, and canned goods such as canned vegetables. Home cooks substituted honey, corn syrup, and molasses for rationed sugar. Vegetable oils substituted for butter.

Food rationing inspired many people to grow their own vegetables in what became known as "victory gardens." Victory gardens allowed more of the foods that farmers grew to be sent overseas to the soldiers. By 1943, victory gardens produced more than one-third of the nation's needs.

In 1945, World War II finally came to an end with victories by America and its allies over Germany and Japan. After the war, Americans thoroughly enjoyed eating meat, milk, cream, cheese, and eggs again. Many victory gardens were never replanted because home cooks could again easily buy fruits and vegetables.

FUN FOOD FACTS

- In 1941, a federal law required bakers and companies that made cereal to enrich white flour with four nutrients that are lost when white flour is made: iron, thiamin, riboflavin, and niacin.

- In 1946, Dr. Percy Spencer, an engineer with the Raytheon Corporation, discovered that microwaves could pop corn. The first microwave oven was 5½ feet tall, weighed 750 pounds, and cost about $5,000.

- In 1948, McDonald's installed drive-through service in a California location.

···· Cozy Chicken ···· Veggie Noodle Stew

Poultry was not rationed, so chicken was used as an alternative to beef and pork. One-dish meals were also popular because they conserved fuel. This recipe also uses vegetables from a family's victory garden.

Time
1 hour

Tools
dry and liquid measuring cups

measuring spoons

cutting board

paring knife

wax paper

large pot or Dutch oven

wooden spoon

slotted spoon

small bowl

Makes
4 to 6 servings

Ingredients

1   medium onion

2   boneless, skinless chicken breast halves

1   teaspoon salt

¼   teaspoon pepper

3   tablespoons olive oil

4   cups chicken broth

1   16-ounce can crushed tomatoes

1   16-ounce can cream-style corn

1   bay leaf

1   small zucchini

1   small yellow squash

1   cup egg noodles

Steps

1. Remove the papery skin from the onion. Cut the onion in half. Lay the halves flat side down on the cutting board, chop into small pieces, and set aside. On the cutting board, cut the chicken into 2-inch cubes, making sure to trim any excess fat off with the knife.

2. Place the chicken cubes on a sheet of wax paper and sprinkle with salt and pepper. Wash the cutting board and knife thoroughly with hot soapy water.

3. Preheat the large pot or Dutch oven for 2 minutes on medium heat. Add 2 tablespoons of the olive oil to the pot.

4. Sauté the chicken pieces for about 5 minutes until white in color and cooked through. Remove from the heat. You can check for doneness by cutting the largest piece of chicken in half to see if the juices are clear and the chicken is white in the center.

5. Remove the chicken from the pot with a slotted spoon and set aside in the bowl.

6. Turn the burner back to medium heat and add the remaining tablespoon of olive oil. Sauté the chopped onion in the pot for about 3 minutes, or until translucent.

7. Add the chicken broth, crushed tomatoes, creamed corn, and bay leaf to the pot. Simmer the stew, uncovered, for 20 minutes.

8. While the stew simmers, wash and peel the zucchini and yellow squash. Slice them into ¼-inch slices on the cutting board.

9. Add the squash, noodles, and chicken to the stew. Simmer for an additional 15 minutes.

10. Season with salt and pepper.

11. Remove the bay leaf with the slotted spoon, and serve the stew in bowls.

···· Sloppy Joes ····

Time
30 minutes

Tools
cutting board
paring knife
small bowl
liquid measuring cups
measuring spoons
large frying pan
wooden spoon
colander
cheesecloth

Makes
6 servings

This popular hot sandwich dates from the 1940s. Ground beef required fewer rationing points than beef steaks or roasts, and the sauce helped stretch the meat into more servings.

Ingredients

1   clove garlic

1   onion

½   green pepper

1   teaspoon oil

1   pound ground beef, chicken, or turkey

1   15-ounce can tomato sauce

1   teaspoon Worcestershire sauce

¼   cup water

6   sandwich buns

Steps

1. Peel off the skin from the garlic clove. On the cutting board, slice the garlic with the paring knife.

2. Remove the papery outer skin of the onion. Cut the onion in half. Place the halves flat side down on the cutting board and chop. Place the garlic and onion pieces in the small bowl.

3. Cut the green pepper into ¼-inch strips.

4. Heat the oil in the frying pan over medium heat.

5. Add the garlic, onion, and green pepper, and sauté for about 4 minutes, stirring with the wooden spoon.

6. Add the meat and cook, stirring, until the meat is browned.

7. Line the colander with cheesecloth. Drain the meat and vegetable mixture through the colander to remove excess fat. Put the mixture back in the pan.

8. Add the tomato sauce, Worcestershire sauce, and water.

9. Simmer over low heat for 20 minutes. Stir occasionally.

10. Open the sandwich buns and spoon meat mixture on them.

···· Crunchy Carrots ····

Time
25 minutes

Tools
dry measuring cup
measuring spoons
vegetable peeler
2-quart saucepan
cutting board
paring knife
colander
small baking dish
oven mitts

Makes
4 servings

Here's a tasty way to fix fresh carrots from the victory garden!

Ingredients

5 large carrots
2 tablespoons margarine

1 cup cornflakes
1/8 teaspoon salt

Steps

1. Wash and peel the carrots.

2. Fill the saucepan half-full with water. Place on medium-high heat to boil.

3. Meanwhile, using the paring knife and cutting board, slice the carrots into 1/4-inch slices.

4. Boil the carrots for 10 minutes.

5. Preheat the oven to 400°F.

6. Drain the carrots into the colander, then place them in the baking dish. Place teaspoons of margarine evenly over the carrots. Then, crumble the cornflakes over the carrots. Sprinkle with salt.

7. Bake for 10 minutes. Use oven mitts to remove from the oven.

M & M's Cookies

M & M's came on the market in 1941 in six different colors: red, green, yellow, orange, brown, and violet. Since then, they have been used as an ingredient in recipes from ice cream to cookies.

Ingredients

¾ cup sugar

¾ cup firmly packed brown sugar

¾ cup tub margarine, or stick margarine (leave at room temperature for 1 hour to soften)

1 egg

2¼ cups all-purpose flour

1 teaspoon baking soda

¼ teaspoon salt

1½ cups M & M's

Steps

1. Preheat the oven to 375°F.

2. Put the sugar, brown sugar, margarine, and egg in the bowl. Mix well with the wooden spoon.

3. Add the flour, baking soda, and salt. Mix well.

4. Add the M & M's and mix.

5. Drop dough by rounded tablespoonfuls about 2 inches apart on the cookie sheets.

6. Bake for 8 to 10 minutes until lightly browned.

7. Wait 1 minute, then use the spatula to place the cookies on the wire rack to cool.

Time
15 minutes to prepare
plus
10 minutes to bake

Tools
dry measuring cups
measuring spoons
large bowl
wooden spoon
2 cookie sheets
spatula
wire rack

Makes
3 dozen cookies

CHAPTER 12

ABULOUS FIFTIES FOODS

At the end of World War II, soldiers started to slowly return home. Many women who had been working in factories gave up their jobs to the returning men and went back to being housewives. So many babies were born after the war that this period is called the Baby Boom. Many young families (and couples) moved out from the cities to suburban housing developments where they bought homes and tried to live "the American dream."

Family life in the 1950s often revolved around the television, radio, and family car. The first television broadcast occurred in 1939, but there were very few shows until the 1950s. Color televisions became available in 1953. At first, television networks scheduled programs only in the evening. As television became more popular, daytime programs became available. Millions of Americans dropped everything to watch popular comedies such as *I Love Lucy* and *The Honeymooners*. Also popular were westerns, quiz shows, variety shows, and news broadcasts.

Rock 'n' roll got its start in the 1950s with the new sounds of Elvis Presley, Bill Haley and the Comets, Jerry Lee Lewis, Buddy Holly, and Fats Domino.

Americans drove billions of miles each year in their cars. To enable traffic to move more smoothly, Congress approved the construction of the interstate highway system in 1956. Along the

highways grew hotels and restaurants, including new chains such as Holiday Inn and Burger King. In 1957, Burger King introduced their Whopper sandwich, which sold for 37 cents.

But the American Dream promoted on television shows like *Ozzie and Harriet* was not the reality for everyone in America. At the beginning of the 1950s, black southerners were forced to attend segregated schools, take low-paying jobs, ride in the backs of buses, and even drink from water fountains marked "for coloreds only." Blacks and other civil rights activists worked hard to end this discrimination. In 1954 segregation in public schools was outlawed by the United States Supreme Court, but it was many years before blacks and whites attended schools together, particularly in the southern states. In 1955, Martin Luther King Jr. became involved in the Montgomery bus boycott. In Montgomery, Alabama, Rosa Parks had been arrested for refusing to give up her seat to a white man. Her arrest touched off a yearlong boycott of the city's buses by blacks, which ended in victory. The Supreme Court said that bus segregation was unconstitutional. Efforts to enforce the new antisegregation laws led to violence and unrest.

FUN FOOD FACTS

- A new, quick breakfast food was introduced in 1953: Eggo's Frozen Waffles, which could be heated up in the toaster.
- The United States Department of Agriculture reduced the "Basic 7 Food Groups" to the "Basic 4": meat, poultry, and other protein foods; milk and dairy products; fruits and vegetables; and breads and starches.

There was an increased interest in foreign food in the 1950s, due largely to the exposure of World War II soldiers to foods such as pizza in Italy, beef Bourguignon in France, and sukiyaki in Japan. Ads for convenience products such as Kraft Macaroni and Cheese Dinners (home cooked in 7 minutes!) tempted women to spend less time in the kitchen. Swanson TV Dinners were introduced in 1954; for less than $1 you could heat up your dinner, eat in front of the television, and throw out your empty container. Casseroles became popular, as well, especially since there was a wide assortment of canned soups available that worked well to bind together a casserole's ingredients.

Vegetable Platter with Sour Cream and Onion Dip

Dips became very popular in the 1950s when Lipton introduced its dry onion soup mix. The dry soup mix combined with sour cream became a wildfire success and part of everyone's entertaining menu.

Time
60 minutes

Tools
medium bowl
wooden spoon
paper towels
large serving platter
small serving bowl

Makes
24 servings

Ingredients

1 packet onion soup mix

1 16-ounce container sour cream

1 pound (16 ounces) assorted cut raw vegetables such as

baby carrots, broccoli florets, cauliflower, green beans, and snap peas

crackers (optional)

Steps

1. In the medium bowl, mix the onion soup mix with the sour cream using the wooden spoon. Refrigerate the dip for 30 minutes.

2. Wash the vegetables and pat dry with paper towels.

3. Arrange the vegetables attractively on the serving platter.

4. Place the dip in the small serving bowl. Serve with the vegetables and with your favorite crackers if you wish.

In the 1950s, many Americans ate dinner in front of the television. Swanson invented TV dinners, which were dinners that were quick, inexpensive, and easy to make with minimal to no clean up. How hard is it to make your own TV dinner? Not very. All you need is some precooked food (like leftovers), some microwave-safe plates, and a freezer. Try it for yourself. Using any of the following leftovers, mix and match your own TV dinners. Only use ingredients that are fully cooked.

Tools
microwave-safe plates
plastic wrap
aluminum foil

Ingredients

Breads and Grain Products

rice	pasta	latkes
pizza	macaroni and cheese	French toast
lasagna	pancakes	waffles

Meats and Fish

meatloaf	roast beef	fried flounder, sole, or cod
stews	hot chicken wings	
sliced turkey	hamburger	fried shrimp
sliced ham	sliced steak	

Vegetables and Fruits

corn	broccoli	French fries
carrots	green beans	applesauce
mixed vegetables	mashed potatoes	canned fruit

Steps

1. Mix and match your TV dinners by placing one food from each category onto a disposable and microwave-safe dinner plate. Cover with clear plastic wrap, then aluminum foil, and freeze.

2. To reheat, remove the aluminum foil. Cut a small slit in the plastic wrap. Reheat in the microwave at medium power for 3 to 5 minutes until hot.

German Chocolate Minicakes

German chocolate cake was not from Germany. It was named after Sam German, the inventor in 1852 of the first sweet chocolate. The recipe was first sent to a Dallas newspaper in 1957 by a Texas homemaker. From there it was picked up by the Baker's Chocolate Company and sent around to other newspapers. Sales of their sweet chocolate rose 73 percent the next year.

Ingredients

¼ pound sweet chocolate

½ cup water

1 cup (2 sticks) butter

2 cups sugar

4 eggs

1 teaspoon vanilla extract

4 cups all-purpose flour

1 teaspoon baking soda

½ teaspoon salt

1 cup buttermilk

Steps

1. Preheat the oven to 350°F.

2. Line the muffin trays with cupcake liners.

3. Break the chocolate into small pieces with your hands. Put the water in the saucepan and bring to a boil over medium-high heat.

4. Add the chocolate pieces all at once to the boiling water. Stir with the wooden spoon until the chocolate melts. Set it aside to cool.

5. Place the butter and sugar in the large mixing bowl. With the handheld electric mixer, beat them together for about 3 minutes until light and fluffy.

6. Using the egg separator, crack the eggs and separate the yolks from the whites. Place the yolks in the small bowl and the whites in one of the medium bowls. Set the whites aside.

7. Add the egg yolks to the butter mixture and stir with a wooden spoon. Add the vanilla extract and cooled chocolate. Continue stirring until well combined.

Time

30 minutes to prepare
plus
30 minutes to bake

Tools

dry and liquid measuring cups

measuring spoons

2 muffin tins

24 cupcake liners

2-quart saucepan

wooden spoon

large mixing bowl

hand-held electric mixer

egg separator

small bowl

2 medium bowls

wire whip

rubber spatula

ice cream scoop

oven mitts

toothpick

wire rack

Makes

24 cupcakes

8. In the other medium bowl, combine the flour, baking soda, and salt. Use the wire whip to mix thoroughly.

9. Add some of the flour mixture and then some of the buttermilk to the butter-chocolate mixture, and stir with a wooden spoon. Repeat until all the flour and buttermilk are stirred into the butter-chocolate mixture. Stir until a thick, velvety batter is formed. Do not overmix!

10. Clean and dry the beaters of the hand-held electric mixer. Then beat the egg whites until they are fluffy and stiff peaks form. Fold the egg whites into the cake batter with a rubber spatula.

11. Scoop the batter into the lined muffin tins with an ice cream scoop or a ⅓-cup dry measure.

12. Bake for 25 to 30 minutes or until a toothpick inserted in the middle of a minicake comes out clean. Using oven mitts, remove the cupcakes from the oven.

13. Cool the cakes on a wire rack and spread with Coco-Nutty Pecan Frosting (next recipe).

Coco-Nutty Pecan Frosting

Ingredients

1 cup pecans

2 eggs

1 cup evaporated milk

1 cup sugar

½ cup (1 stick) margarine

1 teaspoon coconut extract

1⅓ cups flaked sweetened coconut

Steps

1. Using the knife on the cutting board, chop the pecans into very small pieces.

2. Separate the yolks from the egg whites using the egg separator over a bowl. Place the egg yolks into a small cup and freeze the egg whites to use in another recipe.

3. In the saucepan, cook the evaporated milk, sugar, egg yolks, margarine, and coconut extract over medium heat for about 15 minutes, stirring constantly with a wooden spoon until the mixture has thickened.

4. Remove the frosting from the heat. Stir in the coconut and pecan pieces. Pour the frosting into the other bowl.

5. Allow the frosting to cool in the refrigerator for 1 hour. Spread on the top of the German Chocolate Minicakes (page 137) with a rubber spatula.

Time
20 minutes to prepare plus
1 hour to cool

Tools
dry and liquid measuring cups

measuring spoons

cutting board

paring knife

egg separator

2 small bowls

2 small cups

2-quart saucepan

wooden spoon

rubber spatula

Makes
2 cups

CHAPTER 13

SIXTIES AND SEVENTIES SENSATIONS

In the 1960s the largest generation in American history grew up. It was a decade of contrasts: peace and war, achievement and defeat, hope and despair.

At the beginning of the 1960s, the United States was unquestionably the richest and most powerful country in the world. John F. Kennedy was elected president in 1960. He was the youngest president ever elected, and was very active. He implemented new programs such as the Peace Corps, in which Americans volunteer to perform two years of public service in other countries, and the space program, which resulted in 1969 in the first human being walking on the Moon. But the promise of the Kennedy administration came to a close on November 22, 1963, when a sniper killed Kennedy during a parade in Dallas, Texas. In 1968, John's brother, Senator Robert Kennedy was also killed by an assassin's bullet.

Lyndon Johnson, the vice president, became president when Kennedy died. Johnson, who had been raised in a poor part of Texas, proclaimed a war on poverty and pushed forward new federal programs to give medical care to the elderly and the poor. Johnson would have continued to build his "Great Society," but he was occupied by a problem in another part of the world. South Vietnam was facing a takeover by Communists in North Vietnam. Some Americans feared that if South Vietnam fell to the Communists, other countries would, too. After first sending troops as "advisers" to help train the South Vietnamese military, the United States sent in regular troops beginning in 1965. The Vietnam war escalated into the 1970s (by 1973 a truce was reached).

Richard Nixon became president in 1968 and was reelected in 1972. But two years later he became the only U.S. president to resign the presidency. Nixon had been involved in a scandal known as Watergate, and chose to resign before he could be removed from office.

In 1964, the Civil Rights Act was passed. This federal law forbade many of the types of discrimination that blacks faced, particularly in the southern states. Martin Luther King Jr., a leader of the civil rights movement in the South, used nonviolent methods to bring attention to the plight of blacks who were routinely denied the right to vote as well as many other rights taken for granted by whites. While working to combat prejudice and poverty among blacks, Martin Luther King Jr. was assasinated on

April 4, 1968. About 150,000 people attended his funeral in Atlanta, Georgia.

In the 1960s and 1970s young adults were more questioning of their parents and society than were previous generations. Young people wondered if their country really stood for freedom and equality when they saw how blacks were treated in the South and in many cities in the North. Many also protested the war in Vietnam. Some young Americans rejected the American lifestyle in favor of a new **hippie** culture, as it was called, that was based on peace and love. Hippies frequently wore long hair, beards, and different styles of clothing, like ripped jeans and peasant blouses. An important symbol of this group was the peace symbol, an upside down Y inside a circle. In the 1970s, young people took up the cause of helping to protect the environment. Earth Day was first celebrated in 1970.

Almost all young people of the 1960s and 1970s—hippies and otherwise—enjoyed rock 'n' roll. The Beatles, a British rock group, first arrived in America on February 11, 1964 to huge, loud crowds of young people. Besides the very popular Beatles, the 1960s saw the rise of such popular artists as the Beach Boys, Bob Dylan, and Diana Ross and the Supremes. The decade ended with a huge music festival in upstate New York, called the Woodstock Music and Art Festival. In the 1970s, people started boogying to disco music.

Hippies began the trend that continues to this day of eating healthy, natural foods. Yogurt, granola, and organic fruits and vegetables became popular. **Granola** is a cereal that often contains rolled oats, wheat germ, dried fruits, nuts, seeds, honey, and oil. It is still very popular today for breakfast or as a snack. **Organic foods** are those that have been grown without synthetic pesticides, fertilizers, antibiotics, or hormones. Vegetarian meals became quite popular and accepted during the 1960s. **Vegetarians,** who will not eat meat, instead eat beans, grains, vegetables, fruits, and dairy products such as cheese.

FUN FOOD FACTS

- The kiwifruit was first imported from New Zealand in 1962 and became popular. Many other exotic fruits and vegetables followed before the end of the century.

- In 1962, John Glenn became the first American astronaut to eat in Earth's orbit. During his flight of almost five hours, he performed a number of experiments, including eating food in weightless conditions. Chewing and swallowing were no problem, but he didn't enjoy the food, which included freeze-dried powders and semiliquids in tubes.

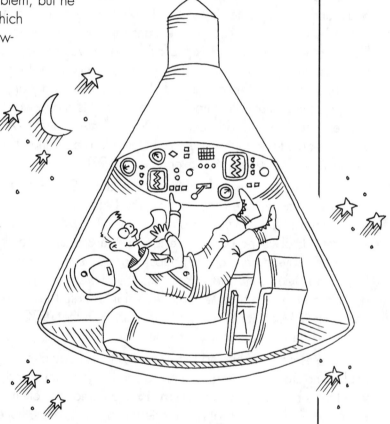

- America became better acquainted with Japanese food in 1964 when "Rocky" Aoki opened the first Benihana Restaurant in New York City. Chefs at Benihana grilled steaks, fish, and vegetables right at the diners' tables.

- In 1970, Orville Redenbacher introduced his Gourmet Popping Corn.

Peace, Love, and Crunchy Granola

Granola has been a favorite of young people since the 1960s. Homemade granola uses natural ingredients that are nutritious and tasty.

Ingredients

vegetable oil cooking spray

⅓ cup canola oil

⅓ cup honey

4 cups old-fashioned rolled oats

¼ cup toasted wheat germ

1 cup sliced almonds

½ cup raisins

½ cup golden raisins

Steps

1. Preheat the oven to 300°F.
2. Line the baking sheet with aluminum foil and spray the foil with vegetable oil cooking spray.
3. Blend the oil and honey together in a large bowl with the wire whip.
4. Add the rolled oats, wheat germ, and almonds to the bowl. Stir, well with a wooden spoon to coat with the honey mixture.
5. Spread the oat mixture evenly on the baking sheet.
6. Bake the granola for 25 minutes until golden brown.
7. Remove from the oven with oven mitts and cool for 10 minutes.
8. Ask an adult to transfer the granola mixture to another large bowl. Stir in the raisins and mix thoroughly. Continue cooling the granola to room temperature.
9. Once the granola is completely cool, store it in an airtight container.

Time
40 minutes

Tools
dry and liquid measuring cups
baking sheet
aluminum foil
2 large bowls
wire whip
wooden spoon
oven mitts
airtight container

Makes
4½ cups granola
(9 servings)

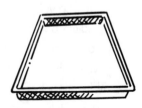

Mother Earth's Zucchini Bread

Time
30 minutes to prepare plus
1 hour to bake

Tools
dry and liquid measuring cups
measuring spoons
5 x 9-inch loaf pan
zipper-lock plastic bag
rolling pin
small bowl
table fork
paper towels
waxed paper
box grater
paper towel
2 medium bowls
wooden spoon
wire whip
rubber spatula
toothpick
oven mitts
wire rack

Makes
18 servings

Zucchini bread first became popular during the 1960s.

Ingredients

vegetable oil cooking spray
½ cup pecans
2 eggs
1 medium zucchini
½ cup canola oil
3 tablespoons molasses
½ cup firmly packed light brown sugar
1 teaspoon vanilla extract

¾ cup whole-wheat flour
¾ cup all-purpose flour
½ teaspoon baking soda
½ teaspoon baking powder
½ teaspoon salt
1 teaspoon ground cinnamon
½ teaspoon ground nutmeg
⅛ teaspoon ground cloves
½ cup raisins

Steps

1. Preheat the oven to 350°F.

2. Spray the loaf pan with vegetable oil cooking spray.

3. Place the pecans in the plastic bag and seal making sure to press all of the air out of the bag. Using a back-and-forth motion, crush the pecans with a rolling pin until they are in small pieces.

4. Break the eggs into the small bowl. Mix the eggs lightly with a fork. Set aside.

5. Wash the zucchini and pat dry with a paper towel. Shred the zucchini over a piece of waxed paper by sliding it back and forth over the large-holed side of the box grater. Lay a paper towel on top of the shredded zucchini to absorb any excess water. Discard the paper towel 1 measure one cup of the zucchini. Place it in a medium bowl.

6. Add the eggs, oil, molasses, brown sugar, and vanilla extract to the zucchini. Stir with a wooden spoon until mixed well.

7. In the other medium bowl, combine the flours, baking soda, baking powder, salt, cinnamon, nutmeg, and cloves. Stir with the wire whip until blended.

8. Add the flour mixture to the zucchini mixture. Stir with a wooden spoon until all of the dry ingredients are moistened.

9. Carefully fold in the raisins and the pecans with a rubber spatula.

10. Pour the batter into the prepared baking pan.

11. Bake for about 1 hour or until a wooden toothpick inserted into the center of the bread comes out clean. Using oven mitts, remove from the oven.

12. Cool the bread for 15 minutes in the pan, and then turn out onto the wire rack to cool.

Swift 'n' Savory Spinach and Onion Quiche

Time
20 minutes to prepare
plus
35 to 40 minutes
to bake

Tools
dry and liquid
measuring cups
measuring spoons
colander
small bowl
paring knife
cutting board
medium bowl
table fork
wooden spoon
rubber spatula
baking sheet
oven mitts

Makes
4 to 6 servings

Quiche is another dish that became very popular during the 1960s.

Ingredients

1 10-ounce package frozen chopped spinach, thawed

1 medium onion

3 eggs

1 cup shredded Cheddar cheese

1 cup shredded Swiss cheese

1 cup low-fat sour cream

½ cup low-fat or skim milk

½ teaspoon salt

⅛ teaspoon pepper

1 unbaked frozen 9-inch pie shell

Steps

1. Preheat the oven to 375°F.

2. Place the thawed spinach in the colander and squeeze out all of the excess water into the sink until the spinach feels dry to the touch. Place the spinach in the small bowl and set aside.

3. Remove the papery skin from the outside of the onion. Cut the onion in half. Put the halves flat side down on the cutting board and chop the onion into small pieces. Add the onion to the spinach.

4. Break the eggs into the medium bowl. Lightly beat with a fork.

5. Add the cheeses, sour cream, milk, salt, and pepper to the eggs. Mix well with a wooden spoon.

6. Carefully fold in the spinach and onion mixture with a rubber spatula.

7. Pour the egg mixture into the pie shell and place on the baking sheet.

8. Bake for 35 to 40 minutes until the eggs are set and the quiche is golden brown.

9. Remove the quiche from the oven with oven mitts and allow it to rest for 10 minutes before cutting.

···· Green Beans Amandine ····

Time
20 minutes

Tools
dry measuring cups
colander
paper towels
kitchen scissors
large pot or Dutch oven
measuring spoons
medium sauté pan
wooden spoon

Makes
6 servings

Green beans with almonds was a fashionable dish in restaurants and quickly became a regular favorite at many family dinners in the 1960s. Here is a classic piece of history!

Ingredients

3 cups fresh or frozen whole green beans

1 teaspoon salt

2 tablespoons margarine

½ cup sliced almonds

pepper to taste

Steps

1. If using fresh green beans, wash them in a colander and pat dry with paper towels. Using kitchen scissors, cut the ends off the beans.

2. Fill the large pot or Dutch oven with water and bring to a boil over medium-high heat.

3. Add the salt and the green beans to the water. Cook the beans for about 10 minutes until they are tender but still slightly crisp.

4. Drain the green beans in the colander.

5. Place the sauté pan over low heat and melt the margarine. Stir the almonds into the margarine and toast them for 3 to 4 minutes, stirring constantly with a wooden spoon to prevent burning.

6. Add the beans to the almond mixture and toss them to coat. Cook for 2 more minutes. Turn off the heat. Season with a dash of salt and pepper if desired.

CHAPTER 14

IGH TECH, LOW FAT: THE 1980S AND 1990S

When Ronald Reagan became president in 1981, the U.S. economy was not doing well, but in 1982 the stock market started to soar. Many who knew how to profit from it grew rich and spent lots of money on big houses, cars, yachts, and other luxuries. In October 1987 the stock market crashed, but because of rules created after the Great Depression, there was no depression and the economy was able to slowly recover.

In January 1991, President George Bush announced that the United States would send troops to Saudi Arabia to push the Iraqis out of a tiny country called Kuwait that they had invaded. Within a few weeks, the job was done. In 1992, Bill Clinton became president. He followed in the Democratic tradition of using the federal government to help improve the lives of Americans.

In the 1980s, many Americans realized the health benefits of exercising and started jogging, lifting weights, and joining health spas. Many also became obsessed with losing weight.

Reports on food and nutrition in the media became more and more commonplace in the 1980s and 1990s. By the 1990s, many Americans were counting grams of fat rather than calories, and food store shelves were loaded with low-fat and nonfat foods. New food labeling laws in 1994 made it easier to see how many calories and grams of fat are in packaged foods. By the end of the 1990s, nutritionists told us that the *amount* of fat that you eat, is not as important as the *types* of fats that you eat. The new Food Guide Pyramid emphasized grains (preferably whole grains), fruits, and vegetables. Little wonder that vegetarian eating has become more popular than ever!

In the 1980s and 1990s, food lovers, also called foodies, learned all about foreign cuisines and exotic ingredients. They knew the names of the most famous chefs and restaurants in the country. Many average Americans also became more sophisticated in terms of their food knowledge and tastes. In 1993, the Food Network went on the air twenty-four hours a day with programs devoted to food and cooking, and chefs such as Emeril Lagasse became household names.

Foods from around the world were showcased in many restaurants and became part of daily life for many Americans. Foods from Latin America, Asia, and the Mediterranean became popular. Sushi bars sprang up everywhere, and Pacific Rim

FUN FOOD FACTS

- In the 1980s, M & M's were taken on board spaceships for U.S. astronauts, and in 1995 blue M & M's replaced the tan-colored candies introduced in 1949.

- Baseball stadiums have always been known for their peanuts, popcorn, hotdogs, and Cracker Jacks. But these days more ballparks are offering local dishes and gourmet foods, as well as low-fat and vegetarian fare. In Los Angeles, Dodger Stadium offers fast-food Japanese. San Francisco's 3Com Park has tofu hot dogs and a forty-clove garlic chicken sandwich on the menu. In the Northeast, sausages are a best-seller at Yankee Stadium and clam chowder is popular at Boston's Fenway Park.

cooking was invented—Asian spice with fresh Californian and Hawaiian flavors. Americans also enjoyed their comfort foods— the foods they grew up with—such as meat loaf, chicken pot pie, mashed potatoes, and bread pudding.

During this time period, more women entered the workforce. The typical American family included two working parents and two children. With more and healthier fast foods, takeout foods, and convenience foods available, more Americans than ever did little, if any, cooking. At the same time, they had bigger kitchens and more kitchen gadgets than at any other time in U.S. history!

•••• Lazy Morning Lemon •••• Blueberry Muffins

Healthy low-fat muffins were a popular breakfast choice in the 1980s and 1990s. This low-fat muffin gets its great taste from two very strong, flavorful ingredients: the lemon zest and the nutmeg.

Ingredients

vegetable oil cooking spray

2 cups plus 1 tablespoon all-purpose flour

¼ cup sugar

1 tablespoon baking powder

¼ teaspoon salt

½ teaspoon ground nutmeg

1 cup blueberries, washed

1 lemon

1 egg

1 cup low-fat or skim milk

¼ cup canola oil

2 tablespoons confectioners' sugar

Steps

1. Preheat the oven to 400°F.

2. Spray the muffin pan with vegetable oil cooking spray.

3. In the large bowl, mix 2 cups of flour and the sugar, baking powder, salt, and nutmeg.

4. In the small bowl, mix the blueberries with 1 tablespoon flour. Set aside.

5. Wash and dry the lemon. Using a vegetable peeler or a zester, peel the outer skin (called the zest) from the lemon and mince it with a sharp knife on a cutting board.

6. Cut the lemon in half. Squeeze half the lemon over the medium bowl. Put the other half in a plastic bag and refrigerate for another recipe.

7. Add the lemon zest, egg, milk, and canola oil to the lemon juice. Mix well.

8. Add the lemon juice mixture all at once to the flour mixture. Mix with a wooden spoon just until all the dry ingredients are moistened.

Time
15 minutes to prepare
plus
20 to 25 minutes
to bake

Tools
dry and liquid
measuring cups

measuring spoons

muffin tin

large bowl

small bowl

vegetable peeler

zester (optional)

paring knife

cutting board

medium bowl

zipper-lock plastic bag

wooden spoon

rubber spatula

ice cream scoop

oven mitts

wire rack

sandwich spreader

sifter

Makes
12 muffins

9. Fold in the blueberries with the rubber spatula.

10. Use the ice cream scoop to fill each muffin cup two-thirds full with batter.

11. Bake for 20 to 25 minutes or until lightly golden brown.

12. With oven mitts, remove from the oven and place on a wire rack. Let cool for 5 minutes.

13. Loosen muffins with a sandwich spreader. Remove from the pan by placing the pan upside down over the wire rack.

14. Cool an additional 15 minutes, then sift the confectioners' sugar over the top of each muffin.

Fashionable Fettuccine with Porcini Mushrooms and Parmesan Cheese

In the 1980s and 1990s, exotic mushrooms became the rage because of their delicious and distinctive taste. Dishes could now cut down on fat and calories without compromising on flavor. No longer only served on burgers and steaks, these little delicacies were added to everything from salads to risotto. Pasta also became very popular in the 1980s. With over 150 pasta shapes to choose from in the United States alone, there is certainly enough variety!

Time
40 minutes

Tools
dry and liquid measuring cups

measuring spoons

2 small bowls

large pot or Dutch oven

cutting board

paring knife

cheesecloth

colander

large skillet

wooden spoon

4 pasta bowls

Makes
4 main-course servings

Ingredients

2 ounces dried porcini mushrooms

2 cups hot water

1 teaspoon salt

1 medium onion

3 tablespoons margarine

¼ teaspoon pepper

¾ pound fettuccine noodles

¼ cup low-fat or skim milk

½ cup grated Parmesan cheese

1 tablespoon chopped chives

Steps

1. Place the mushrooms in a small bowl. Cover with the hot water and set aside to soak for 20 minutes.

2. Fill the large pot or Dutch oven with water and place on medium-high heat. Bring the water to a boil and add ½ teaspoon salt.

3. Meanwhile, remove the papery skin from the onion and cut the onion in half. Place the halves cut side down and chop the onion on the cutting board,

4. Place a piece of cheesecloth in the colander, and put a bowl underneath. Drain the mushrooms in the colander, making sure to catch the porcini liquid. Pour the liquid into a measuring cup and set aside. Discard the cheesecloth.

5. Chop the mushrooms into small pieces on the cutting board.

6. Heat the skillet over medium heat for 2 minutes. Add the margarine and melt. Sauté the onions for 2 to 3 minutes until they are translucent. Add the mushrooms, ½ teaspoon salt, and the pepper and sauté for 2 more minutes.

7. Add the porcini liquid and turn the heat to low. Simmer for about 8 to 10 minutes until the mushroom liquid has reduced to half the amount.

8. While the mushroom mixture is cooking, cook the fettuccini in the boiling water according to the directions on the box.

9. Drain the pasta carefully into the colander.

10. Add the hot pasta to the skillet. Stir in the milk and toss with a wooden spoon to coat.

11. Take the skillet off the heat. Stir the Parmesan cheese into the pasta and divide into four pasta bowls. Sprinkle with chives and serve with additional cheese.

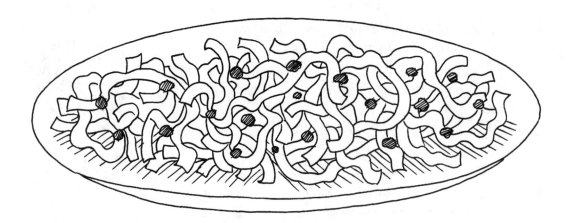

····· Roasted Veggie Pita Rounds ·····

In the 1980s and 1990s sandwiches were no longer made with just ordinary bread. Pita bread is a round, flat bread from the Middle East that has a pocket inside it. It became quite popular during this time and remains so.

Ingredients

vegetable oil cooking spray

1 cup broccoli florets

1 red pepper

1 green pepper

1 medium red onion

1/3 cup plus 2 tablespoons olive oil

1 teaspoon dried basil

1/2 teaspoon oregano

1/2 teaspoon salt

1/4 teaspoon black pepper

4 pita breads

2 cups shredded mozzarella cheese

Steps

1. Preheat the oven to 375°F.

2. Line 1 baking sheet with aluminum foil and spray the foil with vegetable oil cooking spray.

3. Wash the broccoli. Pat dry with a paper towel and put in the bowl.

4. Wash the peppers and cut off the tops. Cut in half on the cutting board. With a paring knife, cut out the white ribs on the inside of the peppers and remove the seeds. Cut each pepper half into thin strips and add them to the broccoli.

5. Remove the thin papery skin from the onion and cut in half. Lay the onion halves flat side down and cut into 1/4-inch slices. Add to the broccoli and peppers.

6. Mix 1/3 cup olive oil, and the basil, oregano, salt, and pepper with the vegetables. Toss with a wooden spoon until well coated.

Time
1 hour

Tools
dry and liquid measuring cups
measuring spoons
2 baking sheets
aluminum foil
paper towel
large bowl
cutting board
paring knife
wooden spoon
oven mitts
pastry brush

Makes
8 pita rounds

7. Turn the coated vegetables onto the prepared baking sheet. Roast the vegetables for 45 minutes. Using oven mitts, remove from the oven. Turn the oven to 425°F.

8. Split each pita with a paring knife to make eight bread rounds. Place the pitas on another baking sheet, cut side up.

9. With a pastry brush, brush the cut sides of the pita rounds with 2 tablespoons of olive oil.

10. Sprinkle each pita round with shredded cheese and top with the roasted vegetables.

11. Bake pitas for 10 minutes until the cheese is melted and the bread is slightly crispy. Using oven mitts, remove from the oven and let sit for 5 minutes before serving.

American Food and Cooking Timeline

1621   The first Thanksgiving lasted for three days! A large midday meal was served each day, with leftovers for other meals.

1623   William Blackstone brought the first apple seeds to America from Europe.

1624   The Pilgrims received three cows (and a bull) from England. They finally had cow's milk and could make butter and cheese.

1691   South Carolina rice growers were growing so much rice that they were allowed to pay their taxes in rice.

1741   New England had such a flourishing apple crop that they started exporting apples to the West Indies.

1742   The first American cookbook, *"The Compleat Housewife,"* by Eliza Smith, was printed in Williamsburg, Virginia.

1797   Johnny Appleseed, whose real name was John Chapman, passed through Pennsylvania planting young apple trees.

1827   The sandwich was introduced to America in a cookbook by Elizabeth Leslie.

1828   The dish we call chili was first mentioned. Chili is made from beef, beans, chili peppers, and tomatoes.

1835   The first commercial chili powder was developed in San Antonio, Texas.

1839   Canned foods started to appear in American stores.

1843   The first hand-cranked ice cream maker was patented.

1851   The first commercial ice cream factory opened in Baltimore.

1853   The first potato chips were made by Native American George Crum in a resort in Saratoga, New York.

1854   Thanks to cowboys, the first herd of Texas Longhorn cattle reached New York. Longhorn cattle were used to produce beef.

1856   Ferdinand Schumacher, a German, started a mill for making oatmeal in Ohio. Until then, oats were considered food for horses only. Oatmeal became popular as a breakfast cereal.

1859 A dependable baking powder, Rumford baking powder, was developed and became popular. Baking powder helps make baked goods rise. Before 1859, much baking powder was made of baking soda and cream of tartar, a formula that did not always work.

1860 By this year, the icebox had become commonplace. Iceboxes had an upper compartment for storing ice and a lower compartment for storing food.

1861 The first known appearance of jelly beans in the United States was seen in an advertisement in New England that encouraged people to send jelly beans to soldiers in the Union Army during the Civil War.

1863 Dr. James Caleb Jackson created the first breakfast cereal called Granula. It had to be soaked overnight because it was so hard to chew the dense cereal.

1863 The U.S. government made Thanksgiving a national holiday to be celebrated on the fourth Thursday in November.

1869 In the same year that the last stake was driven to complete the transcontinental railroad, Joseph Campbell and Abraham Anderson formed a business in New Jersey that eventually became known as the Campbell Soup Company.

1870 Margarine was created in France. French Emperor Napoleon had asked for a substitute for butter that was less expensive.

1874 Robert M. Green substituted vanilla ice cream for the sweet cream he usually mixed with syrup and carbonated water. This resulted in the first ice cream soda, which was instantly popular!

1876 The A & P Company had a chain of sixty-seven grocery stores.

1886 Coca Cola was created by Atlanta pharmacist John S. Pemberton.

1903 Canned tuna fish is developed.

1904 At the St. Louis World's Fair, hamburgers, Hires Root Beer, peanut butter, and ice cream cones were introduced to the public.

1907 The first Hershey Kisses were sold in stores.

1922 A magazine published by the Girl Scouts gave an early Girl Scout cookie recipe—a sugar cookie—that troops could make themselves and make money by selling.

1925	Minnesota Valley Canning created a "giant" for their logo. In another ten years, he would become the Jolly Green Giant.
1926	Toastmaster sold the first pop-up toaster.
1929	Clarence Birdseye developed a way to quick-freeze vegetables. It was the dawn of the frozen-food industry.
1930	Ruth Wakefield made a chocolate chip cookie and named it after her Toll House Inn in Massachusetts.
1931	The first corn chip was distributed by Elmer Doolin in San Antonio, Texas, under the name Frito's.
1933	Skippy Peanut Butter arrived in stores. It was the first peanut butter that didn't separate into oil and solid.
1937	SPAM (canned spiced ham) was launched.
1942	Deep dish pizza was first made and served at Pizzeria Uno in Chicago.
1946	Boxes of instant mashed potatoes first appeared in stores.
1947	General Mills and Pillsbury started selling cake mixes.
1949	The first Pillsbury Bake-Off Contest was held. The grand prize winner was No-Knead Water-Rising Twists.
1957	The sugar substitute, Sweet 'n Low, became available.
1958	The first Pizza Hut opened in Wichita, Kansas.
1964	Nachos were introduced at the Dallas State Fair.
1965	The Pillsbury Dough Boy was born.
1968	Ernie, the Keebler Elf, was created to promote Keebler cookies. He was also used later in a national antidrug campaign.
1973	The first Cuisinart food processor was sold.
1978	Ben & Jerry's Ice Cream started in Vermont.
1981	To respond to demands for nutritious, convenient meals, Stouffer's introduced Lean Cuisine dinners.
1984	New Orleans chef Paul Prudhomme popularized "blackened" fish and other foods.

1987   *Cooking Light* magazine started publication, and becomes the most popular food magazine within ten years.

1990   The U.S. government issued the Food Guide Pyramid, which put a new emphasis on plant foods (fruits, vegetables, and grains).

1996   Girl Scouts began selling their cookies, all sixteen varieties, on the Internet.

Glossary

beignet   A light, square doughnut.

boudin   A highly seasoned Cajun sausage made with pork, shrimp, or crawfish; rice; onions and sometimes other vegetables; and herbs and spices.

buckwheat   A plant that produces a triangle-shaped seed that can be ground into a flour.

Cajun   A person from Louisiana who descended from French-speaking immigrants from Nova Scotia (called Acadie).

canapé   Open-face, bite-size sandwiches, often used as an appetizer.

chili   A Texan dish made from beef, chili peppers, and tomatoes.

chowder   A thick soup made with fish, shellfish, and/or vegetables.

colony   A territory outside the borders of a country that is claimed and controlled by that country.

corn dodgers   Small cakes made from cornmeal that were usually fried hard.

crawfish   Cajun pronunciation for crayfish, which is a small lobster.

Creole   A person who descended from early French or Spanish settlers in the Gulf states, or a person from Louisiana of mixed French or Spanish and black descent.

doughboy   A nickname for the American soldiers who fought in World War I.

game   Wild animals that are hunted.

granola   A cereal that often contains rolled oats, wheat germ, dried fruits, nuts, seeds, honey and oil.

Great Depression   The decade of the 1930s during which businesses lost money and workers were laid off after the stock market crash in late 1929.

grits   Corn that is first soaked in water and ashes, which causes the corn to lose its outer skin and changes its flavor. Next the corn is ground into a type of cornmeal called grits.

gumbo   A thick, spicy soup usually thickened with okra.

hippie   A young person from the 1960s who dressed differently from the average person, had long hair, and believed in peace and love.

hoecakes   A pancake of cornmeal originally cooked using a hoe as a griddle.

icehouse   A room built deep into the ground that was cool and maintained ice in its frozen state.

indenture   An agreement in which one person must work for another person for a given period of time.

jambalaya A New Orleans dish contributed by the early Spanish. A stew-like dish that includes pork, shrimp, vegetables, and seasonings.

jazz American music developed especially from ragtime and blues invented by southern black musicians.

johnnycakes A bread made from cornmeal that is shaped like a pancake.

labor union Groups of workers who banded together to demand better pay and working conditions.

maize A type of corn grown by Native Americans.

Mardi Gras A holiday held on the Tuesday before the Christian holiday called Ash Wednesday, which marks the beginning of Lent (the period before Easter when Catholics fast). Mardi Gras is a day of parades, parties, masks, and feasting.

okra An African plant whose seed pods are used as a vegetable or as a thickener for gumbos and soup.

organic foods Foods that have been grown without man-made pesticides, fertilizers, antibiotics, or hormones.

pain perdu A Cajun dish resembling French toast that is made with stale French bread.

pemmican A food made of dried meat that had been pounded into a powder, fat such as deer fat, and dried cranberries or other dried berries. Native Americans made it to carry with them when hunting or doing other activities away from home.

Pilgrim One of the English colonists who settled in Plymouth in 1620.

Prohibition The period from 1920 to 1933 during which it was illegal to make or sell alcoholic beverages in the United States.

Puritan A member of a Protestant group in England and New England during the 1500s and 1600s who opposed certain practices of the Church of England.

Reconstruction The period after the Civil War when many parts of the southern states had to be rebuilt.

root cellar A pit dug in the ground in which people stored vegetables so they would not freeze during the winter.

sautauthig A simple pudding made by the Native Americans of the Northeast out of crushed dried blueberries, cracked corn, and water.

sharecropper A farmer who worked the land in exchange for giving the owner of the land a certain percentage of the crops.

tamale A Mexican dish made by spreading a cornmeal dough on a corn husk, then topping the dough with spicy meat filling, and then steaming the corn husk.

Texas longhorn A famous breed of Texas cattle that survived in the unforgiving climate of the Texas prairie.

vegetarian An eating style in which meat and poultry are omitted from the diet.

venison Deer meat.

INDEX